Text and photographs copyright © 2020 by Tom Kelchner
ISBN: 978-1-7345955-1-2

1. Cooking — Pennsylvania — Pennsylvania Dutch Country 2. Cookery — American

Cover photo: Joan (Haas) Knechel, about age 18, in 1952.

Generations come and go, leaving behind children and grandchildren and memories and recipes.

The grandchildren grow up and have their own children and sometimes, just sometimes, the recipes endure and cooks say to their little helpers: "your great grandmother used to make it like this."

To Great Grandmother's House We Go

To Great Grandmother's House We Go

Saving 100 years of family recipes

Tom Kelchner

Thomas Kelchner

ACKNOWLEDGMENTS

It wouldn't have been possible to publish this book without the help of a number of people.

My late mother-in-law Joan Knechel is the most important one of course. Everyone in the family knew that she was collecting recipes to write her own cookbook, but it was only two years after her passing that we realized the scale of her recipe accumulation: 1,400 recipes, including hundreds in 14 notebooks that show that she experimented with them and made them better.

Joan's daughter Linda Kelchner, my wife, was vital to making this project possible. The recipes we chose for the book were largely the ones that Linda and her brothers remembered – an astounding 140. That is astounding because Joan regularly cooked that many dishes and astounding because Linda REMEMBERED them. In many cases Linda supplied details of the preparation that were not included in the written recipe.

I can't thank enough my friend Michelle Williams who began a local chapter of the Non-Fiction Writer's Association to give beginning writers the details of the business side of publishing. The first meetings that included fewer than five of us, were held in the back of the Byrd's Nest craft brewery in Carlisle, Pa. We eventually had to find another location when our meetings began interfering with darts games. I miss the beer.

William Woys Weaver, who has researched and written extensively on the history of food and cooking in Pennsylvania, gave me the awareness of what we really had when we discovered Joan's massive collection. This book only really came about because of what I learned over the years from his numerous books.

Joan Knechel, pictured on the cover at age 18, collected, cooked and documented over 1,400 recipes in her cooking lifetime -- roughly between the 1950s and her passing in 2014.

She wanted to write a cookbook, but never got beyond the collecting and cooking stages. Her collection of recipes, in 14 notebooks, numerous community and premium cookbooks and three file card boxes — one inherited from her mother — is a remarkably detailed record of the cooking of four generations of a working Pennsylvania Dutch family in the Lehigh Valley of Pennsylvania in the 20th century.

The recipes came from her grandmother, mother, aunts, her daughter Linda, other relatives and friends. They also came from newspapers, magazines, packaging, community cookbooks and a few from television.

Joan had an active mind. She told everyone that she was smart enough in school that she skipped a grade. She did graduate from high school when she was 17, so, it probably was true. In a later generation she possibly would have gone to college and thrown herself into a career, but in her time that was rare. I believe her interest in cooking, her ceaseless collecting of recipes and experimenting was a creative activity that her very able intellect needed.

One could survey the vast number of recipes that appeared in newspapers, magazines and on packaging in those years to create a picture of what was available to home cooks. Joan's collection of recipes focuses that picture. It documents what one passionate home cook took from the recipe universe — the things that fascinated her (and that her kids would eat).

The recipes that she cooked frequently enough for her children to remember, which we are presenting in this book, create a finely detailed snapshot of the food culture of her ancestors and her own time and place.

Joan never moved past about 1970 in her food preferences. Although she spent many of her final years watching television cooking shows, her recipe collection show that her tastes were firmly set in the world she grew up in and the first three decades of her adult life — the 50s, 60s and 70s. She might have been clipping recipes and exchanging with everyone she knew, but for her there was no such thing as a bean sprout, superfood, hi-fiber dish or free-range anything. The 1994 USDA food pyramid came and went and she never noticed. It was ALL comfort food in her world.

Her conservative tastes, based in the Pennsylvania Dutch food that was always in the background in her area, focused the selection of recipes that she recorded and preserved for us. Only a handful of the recipes in her vast collection would have been out of place on the table of an average family in eastern Pennsylvania in 1960.

Joan was an energetic woman of very strong opinions, which is probably understandable since she didn't have the easiest of lives. Her father had wanted a boy when she was born in 1934 and apparently rejected her.

She was working and earning money at age 12. She was a cheerleader at Quakertown High School (lettered 1949-50) after she moved there from Boyertown, 20 miles away in the farming hinterland south of Allentown. There is an existing photo of her in her uniform as the "U" in "Quakertown."

Joan cooked for a large family — five children at one point— and worked as a waitress in diners near Quakertown. She also worked for a time as a meat cutter in the Food Fair grocery store in Quakertown and had her own restaurant in Emmaus with a partner for two years.

For most of her life, she was the one who hosted the holiday meals for her kids and eventually their spouses and her grandchildren as well as her brothers and their families. She had married at 21, had four children, divorced and had a fifth child to a second husband before they divorced.

Joan lived in a large sprawling five-bedroom split-level home that her second husband built in the mid 1970s. She sold it and moved into a townhouse 30 years later. She soon regretted the move since she could no longer entertain two dozen people at every major holiday. As her health declined in her later years, she still cooked, watched cooking shows on television and accumulated recipes.

I first met her when she was 58. Although my wife Linda (her daughter and oldest child) remembers her as a wonderful, caring mother, she was my mother-in-law and not an easy one to live with. She was a contrarian and always generously provided everyone with her opinion of what they were doing wrong with their personal affairs.

I quickly discovered that two things would defang her: getting her into a conversation about cooking or setting a bottle of wine in front of her. If I did both, it worked REALLY well. When I took over the hosting of family holiday get-togethers late in her life, I found that I could keep her and her opinions out of my kitchen by greeting her when she arrived with a bloody Mary fortified with four shots of vodka.

Apparently, she always was passionate about cooking. Four years after her passing, when we started this project, Linda and I looked in the cardboard box of notebooks, file cards, premium cookbooks and clippings that we got in the "clean out" after her death. We were astounded to discover how many recipes she had collected. Some were clippings but hundreds were handwritten in the notebooks or on cards in file box. Some were dated. Some had the names of the people she got them from. Many were titled "My...," "best," or "excellent."

THEN, we found a SECOND cardboard box in the possession of Joan's oldest son Kenneth Scheetz, Jr, in Quakertown. There was a pile of community cookbooks and two more recipe boxes. One of the recipe boxes appeared to have belonged to Joan's mother Florence (1914-1988) with some recipes noting that they came from "mother" — possibly Joan's grandmother Susanne Rothenberger (1875-1950).

Some of the family's most beloved recipes had been published in a 1983 community cookbook printed as a fund raiser on the 50th anniversary of the Lansdale, Pa., Volunteer Medical Service Corps. There are more than a dozen recipes in it contributed by Joan, Linda, Joan's mother Florence and aunts Molly and Estelle. Joan gave copies of the book to each of her children. Cooks in the family go there when they want to make a shoo fly pie. It's referred to as the "Corps" cookbook.

It didn't appear that Joan ever used cookbooks beyond that *Corps* cookbook and perhaps the premium or community cookbooks that we found. That makes sense given her contrarian nature. She wasn't going to take anyone's word for it, she was going to do it her way. She owned the 24-volume set of the *Time-Life Foods of the World* (pub. 1968) but nobody remembers her using them. On visits to her home I often browsed through them. Sometime in the mid 90s I looked in them to find a Czech recipe for bread dumplings and a marinade for game when Ken Jr. and I cooked a dinner featuring the venison and bear that he had bagged. It was a memorable meal. Sometime later she gave me the set as well as another food encyclopedia that she had purchased (one volume per week) at a grocery store.

It appears that the recipes she she really liked were those she got from friends or clipped from advertisements in newspapers and magazines. Most came from the test kitchens of such food giants as Kraft and Procter and Gamble and Campbell Soup Company. She was cooking recipes the American food industry was presenting in order to sell their products. Many are great recipes. Home cooks across the nation all were cooking them. They were making Jell-O "salads" and the famous "Green Bean Casserole," created in 1955 by Dorcas B. Reilly, a supervisor in the Campbell Soup Company test kitchen, and thousands of recipes just like it.[1]

If Joan had no direct connection to Irma Rombauer (*Joy of Cooking*,) James Beard, Julia Child or Alice Waters she certainly could thank cookbook writer Poppy Cannon for a good bit of her cooking worldview. Cannon was the author of the best-selling 1951 *Can Opener Cookbook*, which presented fast and easy "gourmet" recipes based on canned soups and other convenience foods.

So, Joan's contrarianism resulted in a decades-long accumulation of hand-picked recipes that were crossing the radar of creative home cooks in those years. It's an archive of popular cooking, really. She wasn't going to follow anybody else's cook book, she was going to create her own from the recipes that where everywhere.

No one in the family remembers her going about writing the book beyond perfecting recipes and copying them into the notebooks. Those are labeled as one would the chapters in a cookbook. But that was enough to give us her vision. It wasn't going to be *Larousse Gastronomique*, but it was going to be HER cookbook based on the recipes that interested her — and probably most of her neighbors and fellow Americans — in those decades.

For the last two years we've enjoyed reading the recipes, remembering her great family meals, kitchen testing her recipes and EATING them. So, here's your cookbook, Nanny. Hope you like it.

Joan (rear) and her mother Florence
(Rothenberger) Sell (photo 1980?)

Joan's mother Florence Sell (1914-1988) (rear)
and Joan's grandmother Suzanna Rothenberger
(1875-1950) (photo 1935?)

Joan (right) (1934-2014) and her daughter
Linda (Scheetz, Gartner) Kelchner (1955-) (photo
2004)

(Right to left) Linda with her daughters Megan
Gartner and Ashley (Gartner) Wargo and
granddaughter Jaylin Gartner. (photo 2018).

Joan's Cookbook

Joan (Haas, Scheetz) Knechel (1934-2014) of Quakertown Pa., was married and started her family in the year Campbell Soup Company's famous green bean casserole was created: 1955.

The decade of the 1950s was a particular age for cooking in the United States, depending on how one views it. After World War Two ended in 1945 here was a fabulous new cornucopia of frozen foods, convenience foods and manufacturers' test-kitchen recipes for making meals quickly and easily. Many of the resulting dishes became traditions, eventually called "comfort food."

The other way to look at it was that the 1950s ushered in a wasteland of frozen foods, convenience foods and manufacturers' test-kitchen recipes for making salty, high-fat, chemical laden meals — slim on vegetables and fiber — that soon resulted in an obese population hosting diabetes and colorectal cancer at epidemic levels. But this is mostly a cookbook and you're supposed to talk about pleasant things in cookbooks. So, for the sake of today's health-conscious cooks: ya don't have to eat this stuff every day.

Joan learned to cook the Pennsylvania Dutch recipes that were common in her area: the Lehigh Valley of Pennsylvania. According to Linda:

"(Joan's)... aunt Stella Gift practically brought my mother up. She taught my mother how to cook.

"She was little and she smoked and swore. She could cook and she was funny. She was a sweet, nice person. She called my mother "Bunny. She cooked at the Boyertown Hook and Ladder.

"She worked at the Boyertown casket company — She polished the brass handles."

Also, she spoke "Dutch." That's Pennsylvania Dutch, technically Pennsilfaanisch, based on the West German dialect that many of the immigrants to Pennsylvania brought with them in the 18th century. Some continue to speak it today.

Joan cooked for her husbands and five children and the friends and relatives that paid to live at her home. For some years her home was basically a boarding house. She was the one who cooked the holiday meals. When her children and grandchildren went "over the river and through the woods to grandmother's house," it was to her house. And they usually got a mountain of leftovers to take home. Joan also worked in diners, some owned by Greek families, and she was familiar with the popular food that they served.

From 1991 to 93, Joan and a partner ran a restaurant named "BJ's Steak and Crab" in Emmaus, Pa. His name was Bobby, hers was Joan. He ran the kitchen and she ran the front end. It didn't last long. After it was all over, the Internal Revenue Service had some serious questions about Bobby's bookkeeping methods, or lack of them. Joan lost the $20,000 she had invested, but Bobby took the rap with the feds (as they said in old movies). Apparently, it was fun while it lasted and a learning experience.

Linda and her children Ashley and Michael at Joan's restaurant BJ's Steak and Crab (1992).

The regional Pennsylvania Dutch recipes in Joan's world included shoo fly pie, shoo fly cake, chicken pot pie, Apies cake, sauerkraut and dry beef. After we dug into her recipes and began kitchen testing them, we discovered not only the Dutch recipes, but her spaghetti pizza style, spinach balls, peanut butter pie and a lot of other recipes that were the stuff of legend among family members.

Economy and speed of preparation were important factors in her selection of recipes, but she had imagination and knew what tasted good. She liked fish and seafood, though no one else in the family had her passion for it. Large casseroles that would fill stomachs were central. Desserts were the same. Her two husbands were working men, one a typesetter the other a builder. Her sons, four of her five children, worked at construction jobs, played hard outdoors, hunted, fished and played football in high school and college. Her menus were calorie-rich.

Although the family lived in a meat-and-potatoes world, Joan clearly sought out different recipes that she found new and interesting. She wrote them down and she cooked them. She and I talked about them occasionally.

She was born in a traditional small-town world in 1934, but soon found herself living in a rapidly expanding postwar American mass culture. She chose to limit herself to a range of dishes that resembled what she grew up eating, but her recipe collection shows the vast number of variations that the test kitchens of large food companies were creating and the mass media was presenting to the home cook in those days.

Hers might have been one of the last generations in which the majority of family cooks in the U.S. clipped recipes, swapped them with friends and relatives, preserved them and passed them to their children. Her descendants who cook, use cookbooks or look for the recipes on the World Wide Web. Joan's daughter Linda keeps family recipes and cooks them, but Joan's granddaughter Ashley largely uses recipes from the Internet and Blue Apron "ingredient-and-recipe meal kit service." Joan's other granddaughter, Megan, a busy, working mother of two, eats largely prepared foods, cooking only when time permits. Ashley is the family specialist on cheesecakes, keeping up her grandmothers love of them. Megan continues to expand her kitchen repertoire, regularly makes empanadas and introduced the family to Puerto Rican fried plantain fritters. Those she got from a friend who was born in Cuba.

"Saves time" was the most important aspect of the recipes and products that came from Joan's era. Cookbook writer Poppy Cannon, who wrote *The Can Opener Cookbook,* published in 1951, captured the big influences of the day: fast recipes made from prepared ingredients, such as canned creamed soups.

The book's introduction, titled "A New Kind of Cooking," begins:

"Something new has been added to the age-old saga of good eating. America, never before gastronomically renowned despite its wealth of excellent ingredients, burgeoning larders, fertile farm lands, herds and flocks, has developed epicurean interests — but with a difference. Our cooking ideas and ideals have their roots in many lands and cultures, but our new way of achieving gourmet food can only happen here — in the land of the mix, the jar, the frozen-food package, and the ubiquitous can opener."[2]

The 1960s and 70s were a time when American home cooks discovered the recipes of other countries (first Mexico and Thailand) as well as more sophisticated cooking techniques and recipes shown on television. Americans came back from World War Two with an interest in the foods of foreign places, such as the Luau craze from Hawaii. The trend accelerated with Julia Child's books and television show and gained yet more widespread interest through entire food television networks today. Child's book *Mastering the Art of French Cooking* was published in 1961 and her TV show began on public television February, 1963. The Food Network started in 1993.

There was demographic change too. There were lots of new neighbors from places like Mexico. In the early 1970s, "taco parties" were a new trend. By 2010, piñatas were common at small children's birthday parties and the Taco Bell chain of Mexican restaurants were everywhere.

For a while Mongolian grills and sushi restaurants were the hottest thing on the national food scene, then Thai restaurants, then "pan-Asian."

All that was pretty much lost on Joan.

The recipes she collected, or created, show that she was based in the vernacular American recipes of her day: Spatini tomato sauce seasoning mix, macaroni and cheese, hamburger dishes, use of canned soups in recipes. But she was alert to variety. She created recipes that were her own take on pies and cakes and such oddities as tomato and celery dumplings. Her lasagna variations and many sausage recipes are quite interesting.

The recipes

We've presented a selection of Joan's recipes in this book that reflect only what her children remember and a few that were just too interesting to ignore —such as "War Cake" from a 1918 pamphlet cookbook that must have belonged to Joan's grandmother Susanna Rothenberger.

We've included the source for each recipe if we could find it. In some cases, Joan wrote the name of the person she got the recipe from. Two or three possibly came from her grandmother. A lot came from her mother and aunts. It seems the most came from her daughter Linda. That makes sense because Joan was clearly on the lookout for anything new that was in the parameters of her tastes— the cooking of the 1930s through about 1970.

Linda lived in other regions of Pennsylvania and in Colorado and came into contact with other cooks her age who were also swapping recipes. She was basically the most well-traveled of Joan's contributors.

She also was a vital resource in the writing of this book since she remembered the fine details of many recipes (such as German Potato Filling). She also remembered how to make some favorite family dishes that Joan apparently made from memory, since we found no recipes for them.

We have presented photos of the finished dishes and photos of most of the original recipes. The recipes have a certain historical significance, plus they're just plain interesting. We presented them in color to show Joan's red underlining, her (or her mother's or her grandmother's) handwriting and the wonderful yellow color of aging paper or card stock and of course the cooking stains.

We resisted the temptation to "tweak" ingredients or directions using our more modern sensibilities. In some cases, the recipes that she captured might seem very plain to modern cooks. We think there is a value in preserving the originals. They're "just like mother made," for better or worse. And that's what this book is all about.

CONTENTS

CONTENTS

1

Appetizers

Ring Bologna and Cheese

This appetizer comes from no recipe. Plates of sliced ring bologna, cheese cubes and yellow mustard were at every gathering in Joan's lifetime, according to Linda. Ring bologna also served well in kids' school lunches and on picnics. It was not uncommon to see it served with Ritz crackers.

Ring Bologna is a smoked beef and pork sausage, about two inches in diameter. It has a thick skin on it that is removed before the sausage is sliced and arranged on the serving plate. It is made and sold by butcher shops and small meat processors throughout central and eastern Pennsylvania. Apparently, it's popular in Ohio and other parts of the Midwest as well. It appears to be one of those foods and recipes that had roots in the lands that became Germany and came to the U.S. with immigrants in the 18th and 19th centuries. In Germany today a variety of sausages are made in the same "ring" shape and as thick as the Pennsylvania variety.

The cheese that Joan usually served, cut in cubes, was cheddar, Swiss or Colby.

In Joan's household, ring Bologna was a staple. It kept in the refrigerator quite well since it was smoked.

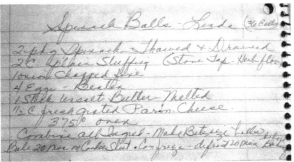

Spinach Balls

(Notebook 1, pp 54, Cards #3)

Joan got this recipe from Linda. It was a family favorite at holidays for many years and it's had a revival since we found the old recipe.

As loath as I am to use prepared ingredients, I must admit that the prepared stuffing mix works quite well for these.

It is important to squeeze the water out of the thawed spinach.

Preheat oven to: 375 degrees

Ingredients:

2 10-ounce packages of frozen spinach, thawed to room temperature and drained. Drain in colander and squeeze slightly to remove the water.

2 cups (1 package) stuffing mix. Joan liked Stove Top brand with herb flavoring

1 cup onion chopped finely

4 eggs, beaten

1/2 cup butter, melted

1/2 cup freshly grated Parmesan cheese

Directions:

Combine all ingredients.

Wet your hands under the tap and form into balls the size of golf balls. Bake at 375 degrees on a greased baking sheet for 20 minutes. They will brown on the bottom, so, turn after 15 minutes.

OR: To make smaller ones, roll into balls 1 1/2 inches in diameter and bake at 375 degrees for 15 minutes, turning after 10.

These can be served hot or cold. Joan added a note that they could be made up into balls then frozen. In which case she suggested that they be defrosted for 20 minutes before baking.

Bourbon Hot Dog Appetizer

(Cards #2 and *Corps* cookbook, pp 2)

Linda and I both remember encountering these, but neither of us can remember where or when. Joan had a recipe in her card box #1, which may have belonged to her mother and grandmother before her. It was on a page torn from the *Corps* cookbook, which noted that it was contributed by Nancy Taylor, with an asterisk drawn next to it.

We have no idea why she called them "Bourbon balls," a name which is commonly accepted as the name of a type of chocolate fudge balls with Bourbon in them. Possibly she simply made a mistake when she wrote the title.

The invention of the real Bourbon ball is generally credited to Ruth Hanly Booe of Rebecca Ruth Candy in Frankfort, Ky., in 1938.[3] The company, established in 1919, still exists.

Joan had a recipe for a confection similar to the real Bourbon Ball: "Booze Balls" (see desserts).

Preheat oven to: 350 degrees

Ingredients:
1 pound hot dogs, cut in quarters
3/4 cup Bourbon
1/2 cup brown sugar
1 1/2 cup ketchup
1 1/2 tsp rosemary

Directions:
Mix all the ingredients in an oven-proof baking dish and bake for one hour at 350 degrees. Serve on toothpicks.

Cheese Balls

(Cards #1 and #2)

It appears that this recipe came from someone named Betty Shearer and it got around.

Joan gave it to her mother Florence. In Florence's recipe box (#1) we found two copies of the same recipe, one with "Joan" and a second with "Betty Shearer" on the upper right corner. The recipe in Joan's card file lists "Betty Shearer."

Ingredients:
2 eight-ounce packages cream cheese at room temperature
2 pounds Velveeta cheese at room temperature
2 cloves garlic, finely minced
1 cup pecans or walnuts chopped finely
chili powder

Directions:
Mix well the cream cheese, Velveeta and garlic. Then, mix in the chopped nuts.
Spread on a piece of wax paper and roll up to form a cylinder. Refrigerate 1-2 hours to solidify.
Unroll the wax paper, coat the cylinder heavily with chili powder and place on a serving platter.
Serve with crackers or bread.

Dry Beef Cream Cheese Appetizer

Joan had no recipe for these but there are only three ingredients including the local Kelchner's horseradish. Kelchner's began selling prepared horseradish in 1938 in Dublin, Pa.,[4] nine miles southeast of Quakertown. In 2009 the firm was purchased by Silver Spring Foods of Eau Clare, Wis., a maker of prepared horseradish, founded by Ellis Huntsinger in 1929.[5]

Ingredients:
1/4 pound dry beef
6 ounces cream cheese at room temperature
2-3 tbsp prepared horseradish
Scallions

Directions:
Mix the cream cheese and horseradish thoroughly
Place a piece of dry beef on a cutting board, spread with two tablespoons of the cheese filling. Lay a scallion on top of the cheese. Roll up with the scallion and main part of the filling in the center.
Slice in 1 1/2-inch pieces and serve with tooth picks.

2

Sandwiches

Rachel Sandwich

Linda remembered Joan ordering these when she went to the Pub Restaurant on Route 309 in Quakertown. They were one of her favorites.

They are quite simple, but the secret is to squeeze as much liquid from the sauerkraut as possible so it doesn't dissolve the toast. Assembling the sandwiches then microwaving them doesn't work as well as heating the meat, cheese and sauerkraut as the bread toasts, then putting them together.

They are best if made on the most sour sourdough rye bread (with caraway seeds) you can find. You can use more or less turkey breast and cheese to fit your taste, and appetite.

Ingredients:
2 slices of rye bread — good sourdough rye bread with caraway seeds
2-4 slices of Swiss cheese
2-4 slices of smoked turkey breast
1/2 cup sauerkraut, squeezed dry
2 tbsp Russian dressing
1 good dill pickle

Directions:
Place the bread in toaster and begin toasting it.
Place sauerkraut in a bowl and heat in microwave.

Pile the turkey breast slices on a plate, top with the Swiss cheese and heat in microwave until the cheese begins to melt.

When the bread is toasted, spread both slices with the Russian dressing, put the turkey breast and cheese on one half, cover with sauerkraut and top with the second slice of bread.

Serve with a dill pickle.

Hot Roast Beef Sandwich

This is serious diner food. There's no recipe, it's just a way to use leftovers: leftover roast beef heated with leftover beef gravy on a piece of bread topped with a second piece of bread topped with more beef and gravy.

According to Linda, in Joan's world it usually was served with leftover mashed potatoes and leftover vegetables.

Burgers

(Cards #2)

Hamburgers, the national dish of the U.S., are believed to be descended from German "Hamburger steaks" and only became popular here in the 1920s after food sanitation laws cleaned up commercial ground beef.

Although the 1906 Pure Food and Drug Act was put in place to prevent the sale of spoiled, adulterated or chemically treated food (like the burger and sausage of the day), consumers continued to avoid ground meat products anyway. It was important in that day to actually WATCH the butcher grind the meat.

It took a major marketing campaign by the White Castle System of Eating Houses of Wichita, Kan., starting in 1921, to finally make burgers acceptable. White Castle sold them for five cents (72 cents in 2020 dollars). Legend has it that it was a White Castle cook who invented the idea of serving the burger on a bun.[6]

The oldest newspaper mention we could find of "Hamburger steak" was in an 1873 news story comparing Delmonico's and Dieter's restaurants in Brooklyn, NY.[7] It was called "Hamburg beefsteak" and "Hamburger beef steak."

Here is an 1885 recipe from the *Lancaster New Era* of Lancaster, Pennsylvania:

> ## *A Hamburger Steak. From the Caterer.*
>
> *In the first place the steak must be good. Any economy practiced in this respect toward the Hamburger will be just as fatal to Its excellence as to that of any other mode of cooking a steak. A good sirloin or a good rump, entirely free from any stringiness, should be used, and the proportion of fat to lean, to please most tastes, would probably be one fourth, or perhaps a little less, of the former and three fourths of the latter.*
>
> *The meat should be minced very finely and seasoned thus: For each half pound of the meat add two teaspoonfuls of finely-minced onion, a half of a clove of garlic, also chopped very fine, and pepper and salt, a half a teaspoonful of each of the two latter would probably suit most palates.*
>
> *After the seasoning is thoroughly mixed through it, the meat is to be formed into rather thin cakes and fried on both sides in butter, the pan of course being thoroughly heated before the meat is put in; when done, dish up and serve with the gravy poured over it, garnishing with Lyonnaise potatoes.*
>
> *Many persons may object to the addition of garlic and onion, and the steak can, of course, be prepared without them; yet in that case it is hardly entitled to the name of Hamburger.*[8]

This recipe bears a strong resemblance to what is today called "Salisbury Steak." (See index for Joan's recipe).

Ingredients:
2 slices of bread cut in small pieces
1/3 cup milk
1/4 cup ketchup
1/4 cup onion, chopped finely
1 tsp salt
2 tsp horseradish
2 tsp Worcestershire sauce
1 tsp mustard
1 1/2 pound ground beef

Directions:
Combine all the ingredients except the beef. Add the ground beef and mix well.
Form into six patties and fry or grill.

Pork Roll Sandwich

Taylor Pork Roll (also called Taylor ham) is a regional meat product that is at home on Long Island, New Jersey and the Allentown area, including Quakertown. Linda remembers Joan making sandwiches with the seasoned ground pork slices and topping them with lettuce and tomato.

Directions:

In a large frying pan, brown two 1/4-inch thick slices of pork roll. Put them on a sliced hard roll with mayonnaise, lettuce and tomato.

Variations we've heard of include adding American cheese on top of the pork roll and spreading the roll with brown mustard instead of mayonnaise.

3

Soups

Soup is the one class of food that suffered the most from the convenience food revolution. It SEEMS like it can be made with cheap or leftover ingredients and is simple. It can't and it isn't.

Really good soup stock IS soup. Soup made with water or an inexpensive bouillon cubes or canned stock is a very poor substitute for real, homemade stock.

Joan made good soup stock with the bones and scraps of meat from turkeys roasted at holiday time. Lacking the holiday carcass, a cook can get bones from butcher shops or meat counters in grocery stores.

Chicken Stock

Ingredients:

7 1/2 pounds of chicken backs

1 large onion cut in quarters

2 large carrots cut in one-inch pieces

2 stalks of celery cut in one-inch pieces

water to cover (3-4 quarts)

Directions:

Spread the chicken backs evenly on two oiled baking sheets and roast at 400 degrees for 30 minutes (or longer, if necessary, to brown them).

Put all the chicken bones, any fat that has cooked out and the remaining ingredients in a large stock pot with enough water to just cover it all — about three or four quarts.

Bring the pot to a boil then reduce the heat and simmer for two or three hours.

Let the pot cool and pour off the stock into smaller containers. (I use one-quart plastic yogurt containers).

Refrigerate for several hours until the fat on top solidifies. Remove the fat and save in a separate container. When using the stock for soup, one or more teaspoons of the fat will improve the flavor.

Freeze the stock and fat.

If you need less than a quart of stock, put the container of frozen stock in the microwave for a few minutes, melt the amount you need then return the rest to the freezer.

Beef Barley Soup

(Notebook 2, pp 5)

This is a unique soup for two reasons: it calls for a mixture of chicken and beef stock and has a large number of uncommon spices. Beef barley soup is quite common, but this one has seasonings that I didn't find in any other cookbook: cumin, paprika, allspice and chili powder. This could be one of Joan's inventions or possibly a recipe she picked up from one of the diners where she worked that was operated by a Greek family.

Ingredients:
1 1/2 pounds beef, chopped or cubed finely and browned
2 quarts water
1 quart chicken stock
1 quart beef stock
1 cup carrots, chopped finely
2 stalks celery, chopped finely
1/2 cup chopped onion
2 cups mushrooms finely chopped
1/2 cup tomato paste
1/2 tsp cumin
1/4 tsp paprika
1/2 tsp chili powder
1/4 tsp allspice
1/2 tsp pepper
1/8 tsp ground cloves
2 tsp parsley
1 tsp basil
2 bay leaves
1 tbsp chopped garlic
1 1/2 cups barley

Directions:
Brown chopped beef, add water and simmer until beef is tender, about 30 minutes.

Add remaining ingredients, except barley, and bring to a boil. Add barley and simmer for an hour.

Greek Beef Orzo Soup

We have no recipe for this but Linda remembers it well. Joan began making it about 1980 when she went to work as a waitress at the Coopersburg Diner. The diner had been started in 1979 by Gus and Zoe Gourzis at 336 North Third St. in Coopersburg. It continues to be operated by their descendants.

If the soup recipe has any connection at all with Greek cooking, it's probably Greek-American cooking since beef doesn't figure largely in the cooking of the Greek motherland.

Note: chopping the ingredients, including beef cubes, in a food processor gives a very nice texture.

Ingredients:
1 pound of beef, chopped or cubed finely (sirloin is nice)
1 large onion, chopped finely
3 tbsp olive oil
2 qt beef stock
1 carrot, chopped finely
1 rib celery, chopped finely
6 oz orzo

Directions:

Brown beef and onions in olive oil. Add stock and simmer for 30 minutes.

Add carrot and celery and simmer 15 minutes until soft.

Add orzo and simmer 10 minutes until done.

It can be served with parmesan cheese.

Corn and Shrimp Chowder

(Cards, box #2)

Joan's son Rick remembers this as his favorite soup. Linda remembers eating it before she left home, so it probably dates to before 1975. There is an identical recipe in the 1983 *Corps* cookbook (pp 16), donated by Roseanne Daniels, Joan's former sister-in-law.

Ingredients:
1/2 pound salt pork chopped finely (or two tbsp lard)
2 cups onions, chopped
1/2 cup celery
3 tbsp. carrots, chopped
1/2 bay leaf
2 tbsp flour
4 cups water (I would use shrimp or fish stock)
3 cups potatoes, peeled and diced
1 can cream corn
1 or 2 cups evaporated milk (for a thicker soup use one cup and no milk, below)
1 tsp salt
1/2 tsp pepper
2 cups cooked shrimp (according to Linda, Joan always used three cans of shrimp)
parsley
4 hard boiled eggs, chopped (optional)
2 cups whole milk (optional)

Directions:
Render the salt pork in a soup pot. Remove cracklings and save, leaving the rendered fat in the pot.

Add onions, celery, carrots and bay leaf and cook five minutes, stirring over medium heat.

Add flour and mix.

Add potatoes and water, cook 10 minutes, until potatoes are cooked through, then add corn, evaporated milk, salt, pepper and shrimp. Simmer until heated through. Do not overcook shrimp.

Serve into bowls and sprinkle with parsley, pork cracklings and chopped hard-boiled egg if desired.

Notes:

— If you can't obtain salt pork, substitute two tablespoons of lard rather than bacon drippings since salt pork isn't smoked. If you like the flavor of smoked bacon, use that in place of the salt pork.

— The original recipe also called for the addition of two cups of whole milk at the end. That would make a thinner soup, which may have been Joan's preference.

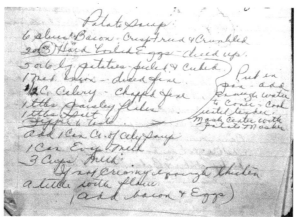

Potato Soup

(Notebook 11, pp 40)

Potato soup probably has been around as long as there have been potatoes, and that's a long, long time. It's one of those recipes that many cooks make from memory and never bother to write down. Joan actually did.

We found potato soup recipes like hers that include onions, celery (salt), parsley and milk in the *1903 Settlement Cookbook*[9] and the 1896 *Boston Cooking School Cook Book.*[10]

Potatoes evolved in the Andes Mountains of South America 10,000 years ago. There were established crops of potatoes in that region 5,000 years ago. They reached Spain by 1539 and went from there to Italy where they were an instant hit with peasants. Sir Francis Drake took them to the Virginia colony and from there to England.

They weren't initially appreciated in Europe in the 17th century. "Moreover, potatoes were denounced by religious fundamentalists because the vegetable had not been mentioned in the Bible."

Rulers in Germany and Russia forced peasants to plant them, sometimes at gunpoint. By the 20th Century they had caught on in Russia, and that country eventually became the leading world producer of them, much of the crop going into the production of vodka.[11]

Celery was very popular in the U.S. in the late 19th Century and early 20th. Celery salt (the *Settlement* and *Fannie Farmer* recipes both call for it) has been around since about 1870.[12]

Ingredients:
(garnish)
3 slices of bacon, cut in 1/2-inch dice and fried until crispy
4 hardboiled eggs, chopped coarsely
(soup)
3 large potatoes, cut in 3/4-inch dice
1 cup coarsely chopped onion
1/2 cup celery, chopped coarsely
1 tbsp parsley flakes
1 tsp salt
Pepper to taste
1 can cream of celery soup
1 can evaporated milk
1 1/2 cups of milk (optional)

Directions:
Fry the bacon and hard boil the eggs and set aside.
Cook the potatoes, onion, celery and seasoning in water to cover for 20 minutes.
Stir in the celery soup (see chapter on sauces for celery-Béchamel sauce substitute) and milk and heat.
If you would like a thinner soup, add 1 1/2 cups of milk.
Serve the soup in bowls and garnish with the bacon and hard-boiled eggs.

Sausage Chowder

(Notebook 2, pp 8 and *Corps* cookbook, pp 18)

We found Joan's recipe for this in both Notebook 2 and the *Corps* cookbook. The recipe in the notebook is different (and better) than the one she gave to the folks who created the 1983 *Corps* cookbook.

Ingredients:
3.5 oz John Cope's dried corn, brought to a boil in one cup water and allowed to soak for five minutes

1 tbsp bacon drippings (or lard or cooking oil)

1 tbsp olive oil (or cooking oil)

3/4 cups chopped onion

3/4 cups chopped celery

6 oz smoked sausage, cut in 1/2 inch dice

4 medium size potatoes, cut in 1/2 inch dice

1/2 tbsp salt

1/4 tsp pepper

4 strips smoky bacon, cut in 1/2 inch squares and fried until crisp

1 can evaporated milk

Directions:
Put the dried corn in a bowl with water to cover, bring to a boil in the microwave and allow to sit for five minutes.

Sauté the celery, onion and sausage in the bacon drippings and olive oil in a Dutch oven or soup pot, browning slightly.

Drain the water from the corn and add more to bring the total to 2 1/2 cups. Add the water, potatoes, dried corn, salt and pepper to the onion, celery and sausage to the Dutch oven.

Simmer until the potatoes are cooked through but still firm, about 10 minutes.

Add the milk and simmer five minutes.

Top with parsley.

Hamburger Vegetable Soup

We found no recipe for this but Linda remembered it so distinctly that it wasn't hard to reproduce. It was a family favorite that Joan could make quickly with ingredients always on hand — frozen mixed vegetables and ground beef.

This seems like a fast-and-easy recipe that shouldn't be given much attention, but to make it well the potatoes and vegetables should be cooked until they are just crisp-tender.

Cooks of an earlier day (before 1970) overcooked food. The reason could have been a holdover from the cooking technology of an earlier age: meals received long slow cooking in a pot next to a fire in a fireplace or on top of a plate stove. Precise temperature control wasn't possible.

The further back one goes, like 1950 and before, recipes call for vegetables to be cooked so long they turned to mush. I've seen earlier recipes that called for boiling sweet corn for 30 minutes (seven minutes is considered quite sufficient today). There also are 19th Century directions for making coffee that called for BOILING it for 30 MINUTES to make a concentrate which is then thinned with hot water. Modern timing for a French press coffee maker calls for steeping the grounds for four minutes, and making coffee in Chemex filter pots amounts to pouring hot water into the grounds in the filter cone and letting it run through, possibly taking one or two minutes.

Ingredients:
2 tbsp cooking oil or lard
1 pound ground beef

1 cup onion, coarsely chopped
1 clove garlic
1/2 cup celery, diced
1 pint tomatoes, diced
1 cup potatoes, peeled and cute in 1/2 inch dice
2 pounds frozen mixed vegetables
4 cups beef stock
1 bay leaf
1 tsp paprika
1/16 tsp cayenne pepper
1 tsp salt

Directions:
Heat oil or lard in Dutch oven and fry ground beef until no pink remains.

Add the onion and continue frying until the onion is soft. Add garlic and fry two or three minutes.

Add remaining ingredients, bring to a boil then simmer 15 minutes or until potatoes are done.
Makes one gallon of soup.

Chicken Corn Soup with Rivels

(Notebook 2, pp 16)

Chicken corn soup with rivels is one of the basic Pennsylvania Dutch recipes and rivels are a true Pennsylvania curiosity to most people. Joan's recipe for chicken corn soup called for noodles, but she did make it with rivels in her lifetime.

Rivels are like small doughy dumplings, vaguely similar to German Spätzle. You make them with egg, salt and flour. If you look up instructional videos on the Web there are several ways people make them, including pouring a thin batter into boiling stock or dropping spoonfuls of thick batter into the soup.

I remember my grandmother, Mary (DelCamp) Leitzel of Kelly Township, Union County, making them. Hers was different than most recipes I've seen. They were much dryer. I was a small child and really didn't observe what she did beyond rolling the very dry dough between her palms. I make them from time to time, but I have never duplicated the pebbly surface of hers. Mine are always smooth. She may have let them dry, then boiled them for a while. By today's standards, she boiled the hell out of everything.

In Franklin County in South Central Pennsylvania, it has been a tradition that the County Republicans serve chicken corn soup at their annual picnic and the Democrats served ham and bean soup. Franklin County has been firmly Republican since Abraham Lincoln was their candidate, so, a lot more people attend the Republican picnic.

When I was a newspaper reporter in Chambersburg in the mid-70s, the story was still being told of the year in the dim past that the Republican women, making the corn soup on a hot day, had so much corn to cut off the cobs that it fermented before they could get the soup made.

Ingredients:
(Soup)
2 quarts chicken stock (turkey or chicken carcass stock works well for this)
1 cup chicken meat cut in small pieces (leftover turkey or chicken)
1 pound sweet corn, fresh is preferred but frozen or canned will work
1/2 cup chopped celery
1/2 cup chopped onion
½ tsp salt
1 tsp thyme (if desired)

(Rivels)
1 egg
1/2 tsp salt
1/2 cup flour

Directions:
Put all soup ingredients in stock pot, bring to a boil then reduce the heat to a simmer.

While the soup is heating, make the rivals by combining the flour, egg and salt. Add flour until you get a dough that is dry enough that it won't stick when you roll a piece of it between your palms.

Roll the dough until it's about 1/4 inch in diameter. Pinch off pieces about 1/2-inch long and drop in a place on your counter that has been dusted with flour so they don't stick together. Continue rolling and shaping the rivals until you have used up all the dough.

Drop the rivals into the boiling soup, being careful to drop a few at a time so they don't stick to each other.

Reduce the heat under the soup and simmer for 15 minutes to cook the rivals and potatoes. To see if they're done, dip one out and bite into it. It should be fairly firm and chewy, but not doughty.

This is one of those country recipes that is never written down. At one time, in families that ate it, the cook just knew how to make it. It isn't a delicate soup, so adding more or less stock, corn, chicken or really any ingredient won't damage it.

Since it came from the days of wood- and coal- fired plate stoves, it can simmer for quite a while.

Hookie House Special

(*Boyertown Area Cookery*, pp 16, Cards #1)

We suspect that this might have been a regional recipe from Boyertown. We found it in Joan's mother Florence's recipe box. There is a recipe (different from Florence's) in the *Boyertown Area Cookery* charity cookbook. The cookbook was a 1978 project of the Boyertown Area Historical Society. Linda and I purchased it at the Euphrata Cloister historic site bookstore many years ago. Linda remembered the soup when she saw the recipe in the book and we immediately made it when we got home.

Linda remembers Joan making it. Joan and her mother lived in Boyertown before they moved to Quakertown when Joan was in High School.

I love this recipe for several reasons. First, it's just a really good soup. It almost seems like the ingredients belong together. Second: it has a great back story. The recipe was submitted to the *Boyertown* cookbook by "Old Sack Rohrbach's Sister" and the book editors mention that "Old Sack Rohrbach was cook at Friendship Hook & Ladder Co., Boyertown."

Recipe from Boyertown Area Cookery.

Recipe from Florence's recipe cards.

Ingredients:

8 oz smoked sausage sliced in 1/8-inch-thick slices

1 cup onion, coarsely chopped

1 cup celery, coarsely chopped

Two medium size potatoes cut in 1/2-inch dice

1 qt chicken or ham stock

1 can kidney beans

1 tbsp sugar

1 tsp salt

pepper to taste

1/4 cup flour

1/2 cup water

Directions:

Slightly brown the sausage. Add celery and onion and continue sautéing for five minutes.

Add potatoes and soup stock and cook for 10 minutes, or until the potatoes are done.

Add the kidney beans with their liquid, sugar, salt and pepper. Bring to a boil.

To thicken the soup, mix the flour well with 1/2 cup cold water in a cup. Add a ladle of the boiling soup stock and stir into the flour-water mixture. Repeat two more times, then add the mixture to the soup. Bring to a boil and stir until it thickens. Do not add the flour directly to the boiling soup, it will form cooked lumps.

Ham and Bean Soup

(Notebook 2, pp 4)

This recipe calls for navy beans OR dried lima beans. To some people, the difference is enormous. Dried lima beans have many fewer fans than navy beans.

It also is important to drain the water the beans have soaked in. Indigestible heavy sugars soak out of beans and that is what gave bean soup its historic reputation for being gassy.

Ingredients:
(to cook the beans)
1 pound dried baby lima beans or Navy beans
4 cups water
(to cook the ham hocks)
8 cups water
2 ham hocks
6 oz tomato paste
2 large stalks celery
1 large onion, diced
1 tsp salt
2 large carrots, chopped coarsely

Directions:
Wash the beans thoroughly and put in a pan with four cups of water. Bring to a boil, then turn the heat off and let them sit, covered, for an hour.

Meanwhile, put the water, ham hocks, tomato paste, celery, onion and salt in a Dutch oven. Bring everything to a boil and simmer until the meat is falling off the bone — an hour to an hour and a half.

Remove the ham hock to a cutting board and pick off the meat, discarding the bone, gristle and fat. Discard the cooked onion and celery from the stock the ham hocks cooked in. Chop the meat into bite-size pieces and return to the stock in the Dutch oven.

Drain the beans (THIS IS IMPORTANT) and add them and the carrots to the Dutch oven with the other ingredients.

Bring to a boil, reduce the heat and simmer for an hour or until the beans are cooked through.

Tomato-Celery Dumplings

(Cards #2)

Linda remembers eating these when she was young and I got the recipe from Joan and made them in later years. It's a fascinating idea: the combination of celery and tomato in a dumpling is very good.

The traditional way is to drop these on top of a pot of simmering soup, put the lid on, and steam them for 20 minutes while the soup is cooking. Add a cup or two of water or stock to the soup to compensate for the water the dumplings absorb and what cooks off in steam.

My mother made plain dumplings this way using Bisquick baking mix. They were quite bland and fluffy. I never thought they were very good. Joan's are much more substantial dumplings and are a great improvement.

It occurred to me that you could also make them without soup by dropping them onto a pot of simmering salt water. Use about five cups of water, salt it until it's the saltiness of soup, then steam the dumplings on a simmer for 20 minutes.

Ingredients:
1 cup flour
2 tsp baking powder
1/2 tsp salt
1 egg
tomato puree
1/2 cup finely chopped celery

Directions:
Mix the flour, baking powder and salt in a bowl.
Break the egg in a measuring cup, beat it well then add the tomato puree to make cup 1/2 cup.
Combine the egg/tomato mix, celery and flour mix.
Drop by onto boiling soup a tablespoonful at a time. Cover and steam on fast simmer for 20 minutes.

Chicken Noodle Soup

Joan made chicken (or turkey) noodle soup with fine egg noodles. Linda insists that only FINE noodles and breast meat be used.

It's a great soup to make after holiday meals when there's a turkey carcass to cook down for stock and leftover meat available.

Ingredients:
1/2 cup onion chopped finely
1/2 cup carrot chopped finely
1/2 cup celery chopped finely
6 cups chicken or turkey stock
2 cups chicken or turkey breast meat cut in 1/2-inch dice
1/4 tsp fresh garlic, chopped finely
1 cup fine eggs noodles
1/2 cup parsley shopped finely

Directions:
(stock)
Pick the meat from the leftover turkey carcass then simmer the bones for one to two hours with a carrot, stalk of celery and half an onion. Strain and discard all the solids from the pan.

For a low-fat stock, chill it and pick off the fat that hardens on the top.

(soup)
Chop the onion, celery and carrot finely in a food processor.

Bring the chicken stock to a boil. Add the onion, celery, carrot and garlic and simmer for 10 minutes.

Add the chicken and bring the pot back to a boil.

Add the noodles and turn down to a low boil for three minutes or until the noodles are cooked through.

Stir in the parsley and serve.

Rivel Soup

(Cards #1)

Rivels are a very old dish and it's unfortunate that they are no longer commonly made because they are delicious. They're similar to German Spätzle, though larger.

Pennsylvania German food writer William Woys Weaver has found two methods for making rivels. The older calls for the egg dough to be dried slightly then rubbed against a grater. The newer various calls for the dough to be rubbed "... between the fingers to form little wormlike bits of dough...."[13]

Linda remembers that Joan's second husband Donald Knechel loved rivels and Joan made them for him. She may have gotten the recipe from his mother.

Linda said:

> *His mother was real Dutchy. Her name was Anna Knechel. She lived in Perkasie. She had a real Dutchy accent and she was very animated. I liked her. She outlived two or three husbands. She had family dinners at Christmas.*

There are three recipes for rivel soup in Joan's charity cookbook collection:
— "Farmers Rice or Rivel Soup," *Schwenkfelder Cookbook*, pp 118
— "Rivel Soup," *Boyertown Cookery*, pp 6
— "Rivel Soup," *The Heirloom Cookbook*, pp 10

Joan's recipe card makes a batter that is far too wet to rub between the hands and it's hard to tell what was intended. Possibly the dough was to be nipped off in small amounts from a spoon full of batter with a second spoon. Or the cook was expected to add flour to it to get the right consistency. I added less milk and more flour but didn't make the batter too dry. I chose to nip off small amounts of the dough with a spoon and drop them into the boiling soup. Although this is an improvisation, it did result in rivels that are softer and have a nicer constancy than those made with a dryer dough.

Ingredients:
2 quart beef or chicken stock
1 egg
3/4 cup flour
1/2 tsp salt
2 tbsp milk

Directions:
Mix the egg, flour, salt and milk together. It should form a stiff dough.
Bring the stock to a boil.
Scoop up a spoonful of dough and, using a second spoon, nip off an amount about the size of a cherry pit and drop it into the boiling stock. Spraying the two spoons with cooking spray makes the process easier.
When half of the rivels have been dropped in the stock, skim them off and put them aside. They are done when they float, which takes about a minute.
Continue dropping the rivels into the stock until all the dough has been used up. Put the first batch of rivels back in the soup to heat.
Serve by putting a proportionate amount of soup stock and rivels in each soup dish.
Serves four.

Cream of Broccoli Soup

(Notebook 1, pp 40 and 2, pp 24)

Ingredients:

2 quarts chicken stock

4 cups broccoli, stems peeled and chopped finely

1 cup onion, chopped finely

3 stalks celery, chopped

1 1/2 cups light cream

1/4 pound butter

6 tbsp flour (for roux)

grating of nutmeg

salt and pepper

Directions:

Cook the broccoli in the chicken stock in a large stock pot until tender, about 15 minutes.

In a frying pan, melt butter and sauté the celery and onion over low heat until tender, about 10 minutes. Add the flour, mix with butter, celery and onion and continue to heat and stir for about five minutes. Be careful not to brown it.

Add the chicken stock/broccoli to the roux, one cup at a time and stir to incorporate it. Return to stock pot.

Use an immersion blender to chop all the solids finely. Bring the soup to a boil, stirring, then turn off the heat and add the cream and nutmeg.

Chicken and cheese vegetable chowder

(Notebook 2, pp 1)

Ingredients:
1 cup peas (fresh or frozen)
1/2 cups butter
2 cups cabbage, chopped
1 cup onion, sliced
1 cup carrots sliced thinly
1 cup celery, sliced thinly
1 can cream corn
2 1/2 cups milk
1 tsp salt
1 1/2 tsp thyme
1/4 tsp white pepper
2 cups cooked chicken, diced
2 1/2 cups cheddar cheese, shredded

Directions:
Cook peas according to package directions and set aside.
In a Dutch oven or soup pot, sauté the cabbage, onion, carrots and celery in butter until tender – eight to 10 minutes. Do not brown.
Stir in peas, corn, milk and seasonings. Bring to boil, briefly, then remove from heat.
Stir in chicken and cheese and simmer until heated through.

Pea Soup with Bacon

There was no recipe for this, but Linda remembered it and how to make it.

Ingredients:
1 smoked ham hock
6 cups water
1 stalk celery
1 large carrot cut into large pieces
1 pound split peas
1 carrot, cut in 1/2-inch dice
1 cup onion, chopped coarsely
2 cloves garlic
5 slices bacon

Directions:
Put ham hock, water, celery and carrot in stock pot. Bring to a boil and simmer for one to two hours.

Strain off the ham stock and add water to bring it to six cups. Discard the cooked celery and carrot. Save the cooked ham hock for another purpose.

Rinse peas thoroughly and add to stock in a Dutch oven along with the carrot, onion and garlic. Bring to boil and simmer 45 minutes, or until peas are cooked.

While the soup is cooking, place the bacon on a baking sheet and bake in a 375-degree oven for 10-15 minutes. Bake until it's cooked firm but not crisp. Chop the bacon coarsely and set aside.

Drain the bacon drippings into the soup, When the soup is cooked, stir in the bacon.

French Onion Soup

(Notebook 2, pp 20)

I've never been a big fan of onion soup. I didn't dislike it, but it just wasn't something I went out of my way to make. However THIS recipe is awesome. The addition of the mushrooms and almonds is a stroke of genius. We have no idea where Joan got the recipe, but it could have been from the cook Bobbie Landis, her partner in the Emmaus restaurant they ran together for a few years.

Ingredients:

6 cups beef stock

2 large onions, sliced thinly

1 cup sliced mushrooms

1/2 cup sliced almonds

3 tbsp butter

2 tbsp sherry

2 tsp Worcestershire sauce

2 cups croutons

1 1/2 cup shredded Swiss cheese

Directions:

In a large stock pot, combine the stock, onions, mushrooms, almonds, butter, sherry and Worcestershire sauce. Bring to a boil and simmer, covered, 10 minutes or until the onions are tender.

Ladle into four bowls, top with croutons and cheese and place the bowls under a broiler until the cheese melts.

4

Salads and Relishes

Kraut Relish

(Notebook 13, pp 27)

This is a very interesting salad and not a common one in Pennsylvania. It bears a strong resemblance to a Russian sour cabbage salad I've been making for many years from a Russian cookbook "*A La Russe,*" by Darra Goldstein.[14]

German farmers were invited to Russia in the 18th century, but in the 19th century the politics of the country soured for them and many immigrated to the United States. Most went to the northern great plains states where they are called Hutterites.[15]

The Russian version uses fresh cabbage and ferments it for three days. It also calls for the oil and onion to be added when the salad is served.

Linda doesn't remember Joan making this but we both fell in love with it. We first tested the recipe the day after I canned that year's sauerkraut.

Ingredients:
1 pound of sauerkraut, rinsed once and squeezed
1/4 cup very thinly sliced carrot
1 tbsp. sweet onion, chopped finely
1/2 tsp caraway seed
1/4 cup olive (or other vegetable) oil
1 tsp sugar
1/2 tsp salt

Directions:
Mix the sauerkraut, carrot, onion and caraway seed in a bowl.
In a separate bowl stir together the oil, sugar and salt.
Mix the oil-sugar mixture with the rest of the salad.
This is best if left in the refrigerator overnight to reduce the sharpness of the onion.

Hot Pepper Relish

(Cards #2)

This is a great end-of-the-garden relish. You dice up all the peppers that are left and make relish with them.

Ingredients:

2-3 quarts peppers (hot or sweet or a mixture of both) cut in 1/2-inch dice

4 cloves of garlic, finely chopped

2 tsp oregano

2-3 tsp salt

2 tsp pepper

Directions:

Fry the peppers in oil with the garlic, salt, pepper and oregano until soft. OR, mix all ingredients and put on baking sheet with one or two tbsp cooking oil. Roast 20 minutes.

Put in eight-ounce canning jars and water-bath can for 20 minutes.

Pineapple Jell-O Salad

(Notebook 5, pp 14)

Joan got this recipe from her sister-in-law Esther Alhum. The recipe has a great back story:

Jell-O was invented in 1897 in LeRoy New York by Pearle Wait, a carpenter who also dabbled in patent medicines. Sales languished for a while since home cooks were not accustomed to using prepared foods. In 1902, a later owner of the company stimulated sales by distributing free recipe books with Jell-O recipes (including Jell-O "salads"). By 1923, Jell-O was so popular that the company that made it, Genesee Pure Food Company, changed its name to the Jell-O Company.[16]

In the generations in which this was originally popular, there was a minor, ongoing controversy over whether it was a "salad" or a dessert.

The popular National Public Radio personality Garrison Keillor did a segment on his humor show "*Prairie Home Companion*" on the question.

In 1980, the dish inspired a novelty song "*Lime Jell-O Marshmallow Cottage Cheese Surprise,*" by William Bolcom. (See footnote for link to page with lyrics).[17]

There is a vast amount of humor on the Web about Jell-O "salads" including a page that begins:

    "You know you might be a Lutheran if..."

    "You think lime Jell-O with cottage cheese and pineapple is a gourmet salad."[18]

The page is on the Web site of St. Luke's Lutheran Church of Buffalo, Wyoming, (originally organized in 1919 as St. Luke's Danish Evangelical Lutheran Church).

If you are tempted to make this with fresh pineapple, be aware that you must cook the fruit for a few minutes first to destroy an enzyme that will prevent Jell-O from setting.

Ingredients:
(bottom layer)
1 package lime Jell-O
1 cup water
1 can crushed pineapple

(top layer)
1 package lemon Jell-O
2 cups water
3 oz cream cheese
1 cup heavy cream

Directions:
(Bottom layer)
Drain the canned pineapple and reserve the juice. Add water to the reserved juice to equal two cups.

Bring the water and juice to a boil, add the lime Jell-O and stir to combine. Pour into casserole dish and add the pineapple. Put it in the refrigerator to set, about one hour.

(top layer)

IMMEDIATELY AFTER putting the lime Jell-O and pineapple in the refrigerator, bring two cups water to a boil and stir in the lemon Jell-O. Cool to room temperature (it should cool in the hour the lime Jell-O/pineapple layer is cooling).

Combine the cream cheese and heavy cream, whip with a mixer. Add the lemon Jell-O then pour over the lime Jell-O layer. Refrigerate until set.

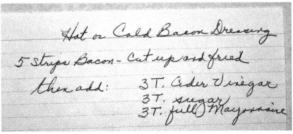

Hot or Cold Bacon Dressing (on lettuce)

(Cards #3)

This is one of those basic old "Dutch" recipes that has nearly gone mainstream. Bacon dressing is now sold commercially.

My grandmother, Mary Leitzel, who lived most of her life in Union County, made this hot, then tossed freshly cut dandelion greens in it. Dandelion is only good first thing in April before the flowers have formed and it gets bitter. And, it is important that the dressing be made, hot, in a frying pan, removed from the heat and the leaves just stirred into it then served. Cooking the dandelion leaves makes them slimy and inedible.

My mother and grandmother harvested dandelion in the yard by cutting a circle around the root of the plant with a sharp knife, pulling out the entire plant then cutting the leaves off without getting dirt on them. The process not only provided the dandelion leaves that could be eaten, but removed them from the lawn where they were considered weeds.

Ingredients:
5 strips of bacon cut in 3/4-inch pieces
3 tbsp sugar
3 tbsp cider vinegar
3 tbsp mayonnaise
4 cups lettuce cut or torn in one-inch squares

Directions:
Render the pieces of bacon in a frying pan, over medium heat, for about five minutes. Do not overcook the bacon, it shouldn't be crisp.

Remove the pan from the heat and let it cool for a minute or two. Sprinkle the sugar over the bacon and drippings then add the vinegar and mayonnaise and mix well.

Add the lettuce and stir to coat it evenly.

Transfer to plate or bowl. Serves two.

Rainbow Pasta Salad

(Notebook 5, pp 10)

Linda and I both remember this one well from Joan's house.

Macaroni salad with mayonnaise, the parent of the "pasta" salad, probably evolved in the 1940s.

There is no recipe for it in the original 1931 "*Joy of Cooking*" and none in the 1930 edition of the "*Better Homes and Gardens*" cookbook. There was a recipe for "Shrimp-Macaroni Salad" with mayonnaise in *Better Homes and Gardens* magazine between 1943 and 1945. It was sent to the "Cook's Round Table of Endorsed Recipes" by Lucy Schurmer Lenden of Oakland, Calif. There also is one for "Tuna Macaroni Salad" in the 1950 "*Pennsylvania State Grange Cook Book*" (pp 189).

The wildly popular "pasta" salad (without mayonnaise as the MAIN part of the dressing) probably only goes back to the 1980s.

One writer has credited *New York Times* food writer Craig Claiborne with beginning the trend. There is a recipe attributed to him entitled "Cold Spaghetti Primavera," that looks a lot like a pasta salad in the article "Ingenious Salads-- Summer Challenge" in the June 25, 1980, Living section of the *Times* (pp c1).

The recipe calls for a half pound of spaghetti to be broken in half and cooked, then mixed with asparagus, zucchini, green peas, broccoli, mushrooms, tomatoes and pine nuts, then seasoned with parsley and fresh basil leaves and dressed with mayonnaise, garlic and vinegar. It is to be served at room temperature. If that is the original pasta salad, it certainly is a good one.

Ingredients:
12 oz rainbow spiral pasta
1/2 pound salami, cut in 1/2-inch dice
1/2 pound provolone cheese, cut in 1/2-inch dice
1 1/2 cups fresh tomatoes, seeded and cut in 1/2-inch dice
3/4 cup black olives, sliced
1 cup green or red pepper, cut in 1/2-inch dice
2 oz jar pimentos, diced, or 1/2 cup diced red pepper
8 oz Italian dressing

Directions:
Cook pasta al dente. Combine with remaining ingredients.

5

Breakfast

Frizzled Dried Beef

There is no recipe for this one but Linda remembers how Joan made it. She fried (frizzled) the pieces of dried beef, added flour then milk. I grew up eating it as well. My grandfather, Lester Leitzel, cured and smoked beef like this when he farmed in Union County, near Lewisburg in the 1920s and 30s.

Although it's associated with Dutch cooking, it actually came from early English settlers in Eastern Pennsylvania, William Wos Weaver, in his book *Sauerkraut Yankees* writes:

> *In the countryside, two taste cultures existed side by side. The first was that of the Quakers and other English-speaking farmers who came to Pennsylvania for the most part from the western England and Wales. They brought with them a cookery based on dairy culture. Theirs was a 'white gravy' cookery, which used butter and milk (thickened with flour) or cream in a vast number of sauce or gravy combinations .... as in 'frizzled beef' (dried-beef gravy)....*
>
> *In absolute contrast to this was the taste culture of the Pennsylvania Germans Their cookery was pork and flour based, with particular emphasis on dough dishes (noodles, dumplings, etc.) as accompaniments to fatty meat. Their brown gravies were usually made of drippings or stock thickened with roux.*[19]

The Knauss Foods company, which began in Quakertown in 1902, still makes dry beef, distributing it the length of the Eastern Seaboard.[20]

Local butcher shops in Central and Eastern Pennsylvania make it as well. We buy it from Dietrich's Meats and Country Store at the Kutztown exit of Interstate 78 and from Wenger Meats and Ice Co., here in Carlisle.

Dried beef varies in its salt content so you must taste it and rinse it lightly under warm water if it's too salty. Be careful not to rinse it too much though or you'll lose flavor. It's made from lean beef that has been soaked in brine then smoked. Usually, it's cut in very thin slices or chipped.

Ingredients:
2 tbsp butter
2 tbsp finely chopped onion
2 oz dried beef cut in 1/4-inch strips and those cut in three-inch lengths
2 tbsp flour
1 cup milk
Pepper
Two slices of toast cut in 1/16s or two biscuits

Directions:
Melt the butter in a frying pan (not an iron one) over medium heat then add the onion and sauté lightly, perhaps one or two minutes. Do not brown. Add the dried beef and sauté it lightly.

Add the flour and stir it to incorporate all the butter, then add the milk. Stir over medium heat until it thickens.

Place the toast squares on a heated plate and pour the creamed beef over top. Add pepper to taste. (This recipe is for one serving).

White Sausage Gravy

This is a breakfast food that can be found in most diners in the eastern half of Pennsylvania. It bears a resemblance to frizzled dry beef.

According to Pennsylvania food historian William Woys Weaver, a white or milk gravy is an English style. Brown gravy (see above), often made with browned flour, is a German style.

Ingredients:
2 tbsp butter
1 cup loose sausage
2 tbsp finely chopped onion
2 tbsp flour
1 cup milk
salt and pepper to taste
2 slices of toast

Directions:

Melt the butter in a frying pan and fry the sausage and onion until it is slightly browned.

Reduce the heat and stir in the flour until it's completely incorporated with the sausage and onion. If it's dry, add another one or two tablespoons of butter.

Add the milk and stir until the mixture begins to bubble.

Adjust the salt and pepper.

Serve over toast that has been cut in cubes.

Brown Sausage Gravy

This is quite similar to white sausage gravy, above.

Ingredients:
2 tbsp butter
1 cup loose sausage

2 tbsp finely chopped onion
2 tbsp flour
1 cup beef stock
salt and pepper to taste
2 slices of toast

Directions:

Melt the butter in a frying pan and fry the sausage and onion until it is slightly browned. Add the flour and continue browning, adding more butter if necessary.

Stir in the beef stock and mix with the sausage and onion. Continue stirring until the mixture thickens and begins to bubble.

Adjust the salt and pepper.

Serve over toast that has been cut in cubes.

Eggs and Potatoes

There is no recipe for this, Linda and I both grew up eating it. It's very Dutch, but as simple as it is, I suspect it was common in a lot of countries. My mother only served it for breakfast, but Linda remembers that Joan served it for dinner as well.

It also was the first thing I ever cooked. My Boy Scout troop once went for a "winter weekend" at Camp Lavigne near Benton in Columbia County. My mother took the Boy Scout motto "Be Prepared" to an extreme and packed my father's World War II sea bag FULL of clothing, food and equipment INCLUDING A CAST IRON FRYING PAN! She sent me potatoes, eggs and a massive amount of bacon. I turned out a quite satisfactory dinner and always remember how good it smelled frying in the open winter air.

In the late 1980s I encountered it at a diner just off Interstate 81 at the Pine Grove exit in Schuylkill County where it went by the name "Large Farmer's Breakfast." You could get onions, green peppers, mushrooms, cheese and probably some more things fried with the potatoes and eggs.

At the time there was a newspaper in that area still carried a column in Pennsylfannish written in the old-style German Fraktur font.

Ingredients (for two people):
2-3 eggs, beaten slightly
2 cups potatoes, boiled (still firm) and cut in 1/4-inch slices.
4 slices bacon

1/2 cup onion, chopped finely
1/2 cup green or red bell peppers, sliced (optional)
2-3 tbsp olive oil
Salt
Pepper

Directions:
Set oven temperature to warm.

Boil potatoes 15-20 minutes until soft but not cooked apart. Cut in 1/4-inch slices. Place in oven to keep warm.

Fry bacon to your satisfaction – soft or crispy. Place in oven to keep warm.

Drain the bacon drippings from pan, leaving about one tablespoon. Add a little olive oil and fry the potatoes until they begin to brown. Add the onions and peppers (if using) and fry until soft.

Stir the eggs into the other ingredients in the pan and fry them until they are cooked through but not overcooked and dry.

Scoop onto two plates and add pepper to taste and serve with reserved bacon.

(Note: there is wide variation in the way this is made: with more eggs, with or without onion or peppers, with a LOT of onion or peppers, with mushrooms, with sausage or ham instead of bacon or with cheese melted on or in it.)

German Potato Filling

This dish is one of Linda's favorites and she was quite adamant about the "right" way to make it. The "right" way includes whipping the potatoes and baking it until it browns slightly on top.

We found no recipe for it but Linda remembered how Joan made it. We got it exactly right after three tries.

Preheat oven to: 350 degrees
Baking dish: 9 by 13 inches

Ingredients:
(For mashed potatoes)
1/2 cup onion, cut in 1/4-inch dice
1/2 cup celery, diced finely
4 tbsp butter
4 cups of potatoes, peeled and sliced 1/4 inch thick
1/4 cup half and half or canned milk
2 tbsp butter

(For casserole)

6 cups bread cut in one-inch cubes

Milk to wet the bread crumbs

1/2 cup chicken stock

1 egg, beaten

1 tsp salt

1 tsp pepper

1/4 cup parsley flakes

1 1/2 tbsp poultry seasoning (or equal parts sage and savory)

Directions:

Sauté onion and celery in butter until soft.

Cook potatoes until they are soft, about 25 minutes, then whip them with half and half and butter. Mix in the celery and onion.

Wet the bread cubes with a little milk, then wring them out and combine with the potato mixture, stock, egg and seasonings. It should be the constancy of thick pudding

Turn into a nine-by-13 baking dish, dot with butter and bake at 350 for one and one half hours or until slightly brown and crusty on top.

You also can bake this in a crock pot (we're assuming you have a crock pot with removable bowl that can go in the oven) then return it to the crock-pot heating element and leave it on warm until it's to be served.

Hash Brown Potato Bake

(Notebook 1, pp 73)

As Joan's recipe says, she got this from Linda. Bacon-flavored Ritz crackers were important, according to Joan.

Preheat oven to: 350 degrees

Baking dish: 9-by-13 inch

Ingredients:

2 pounds frozen hash brown potatoes (or two pounds of fresh potatoes cut in 1/2 inch dice)

1 pint sour cream

1/4 cup (1 stick) butter, melted

3/4 cup chopped onion

2 cups sharp cheddar cheese, grated

1 can cream of celery soup (or Béchamel sauce substitute in Sauces chapter)

1 cup crushed bacon-flavored Ritz crackers

Directions:

Combine potatoes, sour cream, butter, onion, cheese and canned soup (or Béchamel sauce substitute).

Spread in greased baking dish and top with crushed Ritz crackers (Joan favored bacon-flavored Ritz).

Bake 350 degrees for 45 minutes.

Chicken Pot Pie

(Cards #2)

Chicken pot pie is one of the Ur recipes for those who grew up in central and eastern Pennsylvania in Joan's generation and ours. This is the soup-like dish with large square noodles, not the chicken pie with a crust that the rest of the world knows as "chicken pot pie."

Chicken pot pie noodles ready to cook

I'm not sure many people who cooked it ever wrote the recipe down. I watched my grandmother Leitzel make it in the 1950s, rolling out the noodle dough on the galvanized metal counter of the Hoosier cabinet in her kitchen. The cabinet smelled strongly of mace and had a flour sifter on the left of its working area. My maternal grandparents, Lester and Mary Leitzel, were married in Union County, Pennsylvania, the week the Titanic sank in April of 1912.

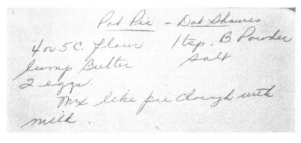

This is a description of the way she made it and the way I've always made it. Joan had several recipes for the noodles (we've included two), but not the entire dish. According to Linda she made it the same way my grandmother did.

In the best of all possible worlds you would use a freshly killed laying hen that had outlived its usefulness. It would be exceedingly tough and would require simmering in water for at least two hours. The resulting flavor would be fabulous.

In the next best of all possible worlds you would use a roasting chicken of about six pounds. You could roast it first before simmering it in the water, if you wanted to take the time. I suppose you also could use a rotisserie chicken.

Ingredients:

(for the chicken and stock)

1 whole chicken (6 pounds or so)

8 cups of water

1 stalk of celery, chopped in pieces

1 large carrot, chopped in pieces

1 large onion, cut in eights

(for the noodles)

1 beaten egg

1/2 tsp salt

1/2 cup of flour

(for the final dish)

1 cup coarsely chopped celery

1 cup coarsely chopped carrot

1 cup coarsely chopped onion

2 medium potatoes, peeled and cut into 1 1/2 inch cubes

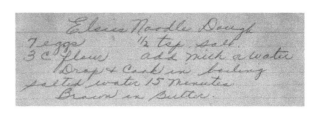

Directions:

Combine the egg, salt and flour to make a pliable dough. A food processor is excellent for this. Flour a work surface well and roll the dough out to about 1/8 to 1/16 of an inch thick. You will need to dust the dough, top and bottom, as well as the rolling pin as you do this. It might take some experimenting. If the dough is too wet and is sticking, put it back in the food processor with some additional flour, or just knead some flour in by hand. If it's too dry, put it back in the food processor with a teaspoon or so of water and run the machine to remix it.

Work to roll the dough thin since the noodles will absorb the chicken stock and swell up considerably when they cook. The leftovers will really absorb the stock overnight.

Using a sharp knife cut the dough into one-inch squares. You can allow them to dry (dusted well with flour so they don't stick to the surface they're on) while the chicken simmers.

In areas of Pennsylvania where chicken pot pie is part of the food culture, you can buy pot-pie noodles in grocery stores. They are quite good. If you use them, check the cooking time before you plan your meal. They take a considerable time to cook, possibly 45 minutes.

Simmer the chicken in the eight cups of water with the celery, carrot and onion for two hours. The meat will be falling off the bone. Drain the stock into a soup pot. Discard the onion, celery and carrot. Pick the meat from the bones, chop coarsely and set aside.

Bring the chicken stock to a boil, add the chopped celery, carrot, onion and potatoes. Cook on medium heat for five minutes. Bring the stock to a boil and add the noodles a few at a time. Simmer 10 minutes then check if the noodles and potatoes are cooked enough.

Add the chicken meat, check to see if it needs salt, heat through and serve.

Optional additions:

You can add a teaspoon of thyme or savory to the stock before cooking the chicken.

For a deluxe version, rub the chicken with fresh garlic, sprinkle it with rosemary, and cover it with about an ounce of finely sliced pancetta or bacon, then roast it for about an hour before cooking it in the stock. For the simmering liquid, use a bottle of wine and five cups of water to simmer the chicken. Use a dry wine with a mild flavor that isn't too tannic. Pinot Grigio, dry Riesling or sauvignon blanc work.

For a really deluxe version, leave out the rosemary when roasting the bird and add a large pinch of saffron (or a LOT of saffron) to the wine and water before cooking the chicken.

For a really, really deluxe version, you can also add 12 whole hardboiled egg yolks when you add the chicken meat. This is actually in the spirit of my grandmother's authentic method. The laying hens she used had immature eggs in them and she put them in the final dish. After they simmered, they looked like egg yolks of different sizes and had a taste that was indescribably delicious.

Chicken Noodle Loaf

(Notebook 1, pp 32 and Notebook 2, pp 28)

This is one of those recipes that was trotted out after every major holiday meal at Joan's house. It takes advantage of the left-over turkey and gravy. It's one of those American standard just-add-a-can-of-condensed-soup recipes too.

Joan contributed a version of this recipe to the *1983 Corps* charity cookbook (pp 67), calling for a bit less chicken and leaving out the parsley and pepper.

Preheat oven to: 350 degrees
Baking pan: 4 1/2 by 8 1/2-inch loaf pan

Ingredients:
1 can cream of celery soup or Béchamel sauce substitute for condensed soup (see chapter on Sauces)
(loaf)
4 oz medium thin egg noodles
1 egg
1/2 cup bread crumbs
2 tbsp chopped onion
1/2 tsp salt
2 tbsp parsley
1/2 tsp ground pepper
2 cups cooked chicken or turkey, finely diced

Directions:
Grease and flour a 4 1/2-by-8 1/2-inch loaf pan.
Make the sauce if you are not using the canned soup.
Cook the noodles according to package directions.
In a large mixing bowl, mix the soup (or sauce) with a beaten egg then stir in the crumbs, onion, salt, parsley, pepper and chicken or turkey. Mix well. When the noodles are cooked, fold them into the other ingredients.
Pour everything into the loaf pan, then bake at 350 degrees for 40 minutes.
To serve, cut one-inch slices in the loaf pan and remove to the plate with a spatula. Serve with gravy.

Chicken Ala King

(Notebook 1, pp 11)

This famous recipe, often served in chaffing dishes in the 1950s, has been around since the late 19th century. Nobody is really sure who invented it. It is mentioned in the December 14, 1893, *New York Times* as being served at a luncheon for Princeton College alumni ("Dinner to Princeton's Football Team," pp 3).

It is an excellent way to make something interesting out of Thanksgiving or Christmas left-over turkey, which is exactly what Joan did, according to Linda.

Although the recipe says to serve over toast or rice, Linda said Joan served it over biscuits.

Ingredients:
4 tbsp butter
4 tbsp olive oil
10 oz mushrooms, sliced
2 cups peppers, green or any other color, chopped finely
1/3 cup wine
1/2 cup flour
2 1/2 cups chicken stock
salt
pepper
1 cup evaporated milk or light cream
2 1/2 cups cooked chicken diced finely

Directions:
Sauté the mushrooms and peppers in the butter and oil for about three minutes until they soften. Stir in the wine and let it cook down slightly.

Stir in the flour and mix it well with the vegetables.

Stir in the stock and stir over high heat until it thickens, then reduce the heat.

Add the salt, pepper, evaporated milk or light cream, mix well then stir in the chicken.

Serve over noodles, toast, rice or biscuits.

This keeps very well over low heat and works quite well in chaffing dishes for buffets.

Turkey Croquettes

(Notebook 1, pp 47)

Joan wrote a note on her recipe for these: "2000 Thanks Sara Molson" which might indicate when she got it and from whom.

Turkey and chicken croquettes are a favorite recipe in diners in eastern Pennsylvania, so they weren't uncommon in Joan's world.

And, they go back a long time! In Fannie Farmer's *Boston Cooking School Cookbook* of 1896, there are 17 recipes for croquettes including a chicken croquette recipe that has essentially the same ingredients as Joan's.[22]

In Joan's household, these were featured in post-Thanksgiving and post-Christmas meals since there was always left-over turkey to make the croquettes and gravy to dress them.

Ingredients:
(Roux)
8 tbsp (one stick) butter
2/3 cup flour
1 cup milk
1 cup chicken stock
2 tsp lemon juice
1/4 cup onion, grated
2 tsp parsley, finely chopped
1 tsp celery salt
1/4 tsp cayenne pepper
pinch grated nutmeg
salt
pepper
4 cups finely chopped turkey

(for coating)
flour
2 eggs beaten with two tbsp milk
bread crumbs

Directions:
Melt the butter, add flour and stir to incorporate. Remove from heat and add milk. Return to medium heat and stir until the roux comes to a boil and thickens. Cool for 10 minutes.

Add remaining ingredients and refrigerate for at least an hour.

Put the flour, egg mixture and crumbs in three separate bowls.

To form the croquettes, wet hands and scoop out about 1/2 cup of the chilled mixture. Shape into a cylinder about two inches in diameter and four inches long. Roll in the flour to coat, dip in the egg-milk mixture then roll in the crumbs and lay on a baking sheet covered lightly with crumbs. Repeat until all the croquettes are formed.

Deep fry at 370 degrees for three or four minutes.

Corn Pie

(*Heirloom Cookbook*, pp 57)

> **CORN PIE**
>
> *"This is one of the recipes I've collected from my Grandmother and other relatives in York County. They are local recipes I've been unable to find elsewhere."*
>
> *Joyce Mann*
>
> 1½ lb. diced beef, cooked until tender, or leftover roast. Add salt and pepper to taste. Line a casserole with pastry. Mix corn with beef and put into casserole. Cut hard boiled eggs over the top (the more eggs the better). Cover with pastry and bake at 350° for 45 min.
>
> 57

This might be a local recipe. It is VERY Dutch. Linda and her brother Ken both remember it and said Joan used fresh sweet corn. I couldn't find a recipe for it in any of Joan's notebooks or cards so I took the recipe donated by Joyce Mann to the *Quakertown Historic Society Heirloom Cookbook.* Possibly Joan used it, or just made this from memory.

The recipe in the cookbook is pretty bare bones so I've filled in the details.

Preheat oven to: 350 degrees

Baking Pan: 8-by-8 inches

Ingredients:

(for the meat)

1 1/2 pounds beef, ground coarsely in food processor (or chopped)

1 cup water

1 tsp beef base

1/2 clove garlic

1 tbsp onion, chopped coarsely

2 cups corn, freshly cut from the cob is best

1/2 tsp salt

2 tbsp flour

(for casserole)

3 eggs, hard boiled and sliced 1/4 inch thick

1 recipe pie crust (double crust)

Directions:

Put the beef, water, beef base, garlic and onion in a sauce pan and simmer 30 minutes. Add the corn and salt and bring to a boil. Thicken with the two tablespoons of flour.

Line an eight-by-eight casserole with short pastry. Pour the meat-corn mixture into the crust and spread the slices of hard-boiled eggs evenly over the top. Cover with the top crust, pinch around sides, trim and cut four vents in the top. Bake at 350 degrees for 45 minutes.

Buweschenkel

(Cards #2)

Linda remembers fondly the times her mother took her to visit her grandfather Myron Haas and the couple who lived with him, Elsie and Kaley, in Bechtlesville about 20 miles west of Quakertown.

In addition to a barn and creek where she and her brother Ken could play, they looked forward to Elsie's "fill't noodles," or buweschenkel.

Buweschenkel are something like a large pierogi with a filling of mashed potatoes seasoned with onion (or chives), bacon and parsley. Joan had Elsie's recipe for the dough but the filling clearly was just one of those things that everybody made from memory. Linda remembered it.

The dish probably came to Pennsylvania from Swabia in southern Germany with immigrants from there. Pennsylvania food historical William Woys Weaver found a recipe for it in Friederike Löffler's cookbook *Oekonomisches Handbuch für Frauenzimmer* (Economical Manual of Domestic Arts) published in Stuttgart in 1791.[23]

In Pennsylvania, the dish appears to be regional to the eastern Berks and Lehigh county areas. There are two recipes for it in *Boyertown Cookery* charity cookbook that Joan had "Boova Shenkel or Filled Noodles," and "Boova Shankle (filled noodles)" on page 22, and another in the *Schwenkffelder Cook Book* charity cookbook ("Filled Noodles Or Boova Shenkel") (pp 89).

You can purchase pre-made ones from the Boova Haus bakery that specializes in them at the Quakertown Farmers Market.

I cut the noodle recipe, above, in half and it made three buweschenkel that are pictured.

When you make these, keep in mind that they expand by about a fourth when they are boiled. The flat edges of the half circles in the picture were about eight inches before they were boiled and expanded to 10 inches by the time they were boiled, browned and served.

Ingredients:
(Dough)
1 1/2 cups flour
3 eggs
1/4 tsp salt

(Filling)
4 cups potatoes, peeled and sliced one-fourth inch thick
1/4 cup milk
3 tbsp butter
4 scallions, chopped
3 slices double-smoked bacon cut in 1/2-inch squares and fried slightly (still soft)
1 cup finely chopped parsley

(To fry)
4 tbsp butter

Directions:
(Dough)
Combine the flour, eggs and salt in a food processor. Add a little water or milk if the dough is too stiff. Divide into three pieces and roll each one out on a floured surface to eight inches in diameter.

(Filling)
Cook the potatoes until soft, about 20 minutes.

Put them in the bowl of a mixer with the milk and butter and beat until fluffy.

Stir in the scallions, bacon and parsley.

Put one third of the mixture in each of the dough circles (at least a half inch from the edges) then use your finger dipped in a cup of water to wet the perimeter of the circles. Fold one side over to make a filled half circle and seal with a fork.

Bring a stock pot full of water to a boil then turn it down to a simmer. Carefully lower the buweschenkel into the pot and simmer 10 minutes. Do not let the pot actively boil.

Heat the butter in a large frying pan over medium high heat. Using two spatulas, pick one of the buweschenkel out of the pot, drain as much water from it as possible, place it in the butter in the frying pan and brown slightly on both sides. Place on a platter in a warm oven until all three have been browned.

When all the buweschenkel have been browned, pour the remaining butter from the frying pan over them and serve. The butter should be brown.

Home Bake Beans

(Notebook 1, pp 80)

These baked beans can be made with great northern beans or lima beans. Joan's recipe has an interesting procedure for softening the beans quickly before cooking: bringing them to a boil in a lot of water, adding baking soda and simmering for 15 minutes. They are then drained and rinsed, covered with water again and cooked.

The standard way to soften dried beans is soaking them overnight or bringing them to a boil, then turning off the heat and letting them sit for an hour before cooking them.

Ingredients:
1 pound great northern beans, dried lima beans or dried baby limas
1 tsp baking soda
1/2 pound bacon diced and browned
2 cups onion, coarsely chopped
8 oz tomato sauce
1 1/2 cup ketchup
4 cups water
1/2 cup brown sugar
1/2 cup granulated sugar
2 tsp salt
1/2 tsp pepper

Directions:
Put beans in a pan with enough water to cover by two to three inches. Bring to a boil. Add baking soda then simmer for 15 minutes. Drain and rinse well. Cover with water and allow to sit for an hour

In Dutch oven or heavy pot, fry the bacon until it begins to brown (five minutes) then add the onion and cook until it begins to soften.

Drain the beans and add them with the remaining ingredients, bring to a boil and simmer, covered, for one hour or until the beans are cooked through. If they begin to cook dry, add water or tomato juice.

Impossible Cheeseburger Pie

(Cards #1 and #3)

Linda got this recipe from her friends Pam and Bill when she lived in North Wales in the early 80s. It's the same recipe as one that appeared in a Bisquick premium cookbook dated 1982[24] and is NOT in the 1964 Bisquick Cookbook that Joan had.

I suspect that the "impossible" in the title has something to do with marketing and image since this couldn't be simpler to make. It is important to mix the Bisquick, milk and eggs until the Bisquick is completely combined and no lumps remain. A blender makes easy work of that, but without a blender it is a difficult task.

Linda obviously gave it to Joan who gave it to her mother. We found it in Florence's recipe box with "Joan" on it.

Linda made it often for her family.

Preheat oven to: 400 degrees
Baking dish: pie pan

Ingredients:
1 pound ground beef
1 1/2 cups coarsely chopped onion
1 1/2 cups milk
3 eggs
3/4 cup Bisquick
1/2 tsp salt
1/4 tsp pepper
(topping)
2 tomatoes, sliced
1 cup shredded cheese

Directions:
Fry the hamburger and onion until the meat begins to brown.

Mix the milk, eggs, Bisquick, salt and pepper until the lumps are nearly all dissolved. You can use a blender for this.

Put the hamburger and onion in a greased pie pan. Pour the liquid ingredients over it.

Bake in the center of a 400-degree oven for 30 minutes then check to see if it is done in the center.

When it is done, sprinkle the cheese over top and cover with the sliced tomatoes. Bake an additional eight minutes.

Impossible Lasagna Pie

(Notebook 2, pp 39)

Preheat oven to: 400 degrees
Baking dish: nine-inch pie pan

Ingredients:
(filling)
1 pound ground beef
1 tsp salt
1/2 tsp oregano
6 oz tomato paste
1/2 cup shredded mozzarella cheese
1/2 cup cottage cheese

(top)
1 cup milk
1/2 cup Bisquick
2 eggs
1/2 cup shredded mozzarella cheese

Directions:

(filling)
Spread the cottage cheese on the bottom of a greased nine-inch pie pan.

Sauté the beef until cooked. Add salt oregano and tomato paste. Combine well. Stir in the half cup mozzarella cheese Spoon on top of the cottage cheese in an even layer.

Put the milk, eggs and Bisquick in a blender and run until it is all combined. Pour over top of the pie filling.

Bake in 400-degree oven for 35 minutes.

Cover with one half cup mozzarella cheese and bake two minutes until melted.

Mom's Chuck Stew

(Notebook 2, pp 50)

This is a layered stew that is made in the style of a gambis, which is a cooking method from the middle ages when cooks used pottery pots in ovens or Dutch ovens over hot coals.

Since the recipe is labeled "mom's" chuck stew, it probably was handed down to Joan from her mother, Florence.

Ingredients:
4 strips bacon, cut in half
1 pound lean ground beef
1 1/2 cups onion, sliced 1/4 inch thick
4 large carrots, sliced 1/4 inch thick
4 large potatoes, sliced 1/4 inch thick
salt and pepper
1/2 cup tomato juice

Directions:
Spread the bacon on the bottom of a Dutch oven or heavy pot
Cover with the raw ground beef and pat down. Sprinkle with salt and pepper.
Cover with a layer of half the onions, then half the carrots. Sprinkle with salt and pepper.
Cover with a layer of the remaining half of the onions then a layer of the remaining half of the carrots. Sprinkle with salt and pepper.
Cover with a layer of the potatoes and sprinkle with salt and pepper.
Put on a hot burner, covered, for five minutes then add tomato juice. Reduce the heat and simmer for 50 minutes.

Spaghetti and Meat Balls

(Cards #4)

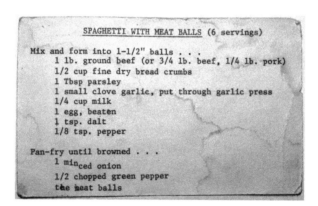

```
Drain fat from pan.

Add and simmer slowly  about 1 to 1-1/2 hours . . .
    3-1/2 cups tomatoes or tomato puree (#2-1/2 can)
    1 can tomato paste (6 oz. can)
    2 cans water (tomato paste cans)
    1 tsp. salt
    1/8 tsp. pepper
    Spatini Spaghetti Sauce Mix (about half an envelope)
    1 bay leaf

Pour over hot spaghetti (1 lb.) on platter.
Sprinkle with grated Parmesan cheese.

6 servings.
```

This recipe came from Linda's recipe box, which she used from about 1980 through 1991. It is spaghetti the way Joan made it, although Linda remembered that Joan always put a half teaspoon of cocoa in her sauce.

Ingredients:
(for meat balls)
3/4 pound lean ground beef
1/4 pound ground pork or loose sausage
1/2 cup bread crumbs
2 tbsp fresh parsley
1 clove garlic chopped finely
1/4 cup milk
1 egg, beaten
1 tsp salt
1/8 tsp pepper
olive oil for frying
(for sauce)
1 medium onion, chopped coarsely
1/2 green pepper chopped coarsely
1 recipe of Joan's tomato sauce (see "Sauces").

Directions:
Combine all ingredients for the meat balls, form into balls about two inches in diameter and brown slightly in olive oil in two batches in a Dutch oven or heavy pot.

Remove the meat balls and fry the onion and green pepper for two or three minutes in the drippings.

Return the meat balls to the pot and add the sauce.

Simmer for one hour.

Serve with spaghetti.

Filled Cabbage

(Notebook 2, pp 44)

Joan always served stuffed cabbage leaves with mashed potatoes. Some of the tomatoes and juice from the pot was always poured over the potatoes on the plate.

Ingredients
1 cups water
1/2 cup rice
1 1/2 pounds ground beef

1 large clove garlic, crushed

1/2 cup tomato sauce

1 egg

salt

pepper

1 large head cabbage

16 oz can diced tomatoes

Directions:

Bring the chopped tomatoes to a boil and pour into a crock pot set on high.

Cook the rice in the water for 10 minutes. Drain and cool.

Mix the rice with the ground beef, garlic, tomato sauce, egg, salt and pepper.

Put two inches of water in a stock pot and bring to a boil. Place the cabbage head in the pot and steam the outer leaves for about two minutes. Remove the cabbage to a cutting board. Cut the outermost leaf at the base and remove the leaf intact. Repeat with the next outermost leaf.

Return the cabbage to the pot, steam two minutes and repeat above.

Take a cabbage leaf, put two or three tablespoons of the filling toward the bottom. Fold over the base of the leaf to cover the filling. Fold in the sides and roll up. Place the filled cabbage leaf, open side down, in the tomatoes in the crock pot.

Since it takes a few minutes for the cabbage leaves to steam, you can cut some off and return the cabbage head to the pot to steam while you assemble the stuffed cabbage rolls.

The cabbage leaves will be smaller as you work to the center of the head. Use less filling for smaller leaves, but try to fill the rolls as much as possible.

When you have used all the filling and the rolls are all in the crock pot, cut the remaining portion of the cabbage head in eights and place on top of the cabbage rolls.

Cook on high in the crock pot until the tomatoes are visibly boiling around the outside (30 minutes) then turn to low and cook one to one and a half hours.

Stuffed cabbage leaves are not delicate. The crock pot can be set on low to keep them ready for serving.

Filled Peppers

(Cards #3)

Joan made these a lot. I remember eating them at her house.

Ingredients
1 cup water
1/3 cup rice
1 pound ground beef
1 large clove garlic, crushed

1/2 cup tomato sauce

1 egg

salt

pepper

6 red or green peppers

16 oz can chopped tomatoes

Directions:

Cook the rice in the water for 10 minutes. Drain and cool.

Mix the rice with the ground beef, garlic tomato sauce, egg, salt and pepper.

Cut the stems out of the peppers and remove the seeds and membranes. Be careful not to break or cut the bodies of the peppers.

Stuff the meat and rice mixture into the peppers. Pour the chopped tomatoes into a large pot then place the peppers on top of them, open side up.

Cover the pot and bring it to a boil, being careful not to burn the peppers. Simmer for 45 minutes to an hour, adding water or beef stock to prevent it from going day.

These also can be made in a crock pot: bring the chopped tomatoes to a boil in a sauce pan then pour into crock pot set on high. Put assembled stuffed peppers on top of the tomatoes and simmer in the crock pot for an hour.

These improve after sitting overnight.

Mashed Potatoes

Linda learned to make mashed potatoes from Joan and has made them the same way her entire life. Any other recipe is "wrong" in her book.

Ingredients:
4 cups potatoes, peeled and sliced in 1/4-inch slices (or thinner)
3 cups water
1/2 cup milk, warmed in the microwave
4 tablespoons butter
1/2 tsp salt
1/2 tsp pepper

Directions:
Cook the potatoes in water to cover until they are soft (10-15 minutes).
Drain them well, then mash them with a potato masher.
Combine the potatoes in mixer bowl with the remaining ingredients and beat them, slowly at first, then at maximum speed to whip.

Potato Cakes

This recipe was a traditional way to take advantage of the mountain of left-over mashed potatoes that was left after any holiday meal at Joan's house. They really are a great way to make day old (or days old) mashed potatoes fresh and interesting. They are especially good when eaten with a bit of sour cream.

Ingredients:
2 cups mashed potatoes
1/2 cup finely chopped onion
1 egg
2 tbsp flour
1 cup bread crumbs

Directions:
Mix the potatoes, onion, egg and flour in a bowl until combined.
Wet your hands and form the mixture into four patties. Coat with bread crumbs on both sides.
Fry over medium heat in one fourth inch of peanut (or other) oil until slightly brown. Drain and place on a paper towel on a platter in a warm oven to keep until ready to serve.

Chili Con Carne

(Cards #1)

This appears to be a very old fashioned or eccentric recipe probably from the first half of the 20th century. There is no chili powder or garlic in it. The only seasoning listed is "...a little ketchup." It's hard to tell if the lack of other seasonings was personal preference or a way of making chili at that time in rural eastern Pennsylvania.

We think this might have been a recipe from Joan's grandmother Susanna Rothenberger (1875-1950) and might date to the 1930s or 40s since it contains tomatoes. (See below).

The handwriting is not Joan's and we don't think it's that of her mother, Florence, either. It was in the recipe box that we believe that Joan got from her mother, which contains recipes from Suzanna, her grandmother.

Joan did put chili powder in her chili, so, if she used this recipe she didn't follow it exactly.

There also is the possibility that the recipe writer was familiar with a spicier variety of catsup than that we know today. Pennsylvania food writer William Woys Weaver gave a very highly seasoned 1912 recipe for "Dr. Esenwein's tomato catsup" in his book *America Eats*.

In a two-gallon batch of catsup it called for six two-inch cayenne peppers, one and a half garlic cloves and 1 2/3 tablespoons of white pepper. That amount of cayenne peppers would be plenty hot and give the chili a significant pepper flavor.

Dr. Esenwein was a pharmacist and patent medicine manufacturer in Reading, Pa. Reading is about a 30-minute drive west from Boyertown.

Weaver wrote:

> *This was doubtless one of the most popular of all Pennsylvania Dutch catsup recipes and one that captured the spicy, West Indian character of the old-style catsups that came into fashion in American cookery in the 1820s.*[25]

Since hot and spicy catsup had been a popular condiment on the American table since the 1820s, its use in a recipe for "chili con carne," created by someone unfamiliar with more traditional chili, or someone who didn't care for chili powder, isn't that far a stretch of the imagination.

American cooks started putting tomatoes in their chili between the world wars (see below), so, the recipe probably came from that time or after.

There is no recipe for chili in Fanny Farmer's 1896 *Boston Cooking School Cook Book* or the 1903 *Settlement Cook Book*.

Recipes from the 1950s until recently were seasoned mildly compared to today's formulas. They called for small, teaspoon amounts of chili powder.

A recipe for chili in the 1950 *Pennsylvania State Grange Cook Book* calls for a small amount of chili powder and bay leaf (pp 147).

Better Homes and Gardens New Cookbook 1976 edition (pp 196) has a recipe that also calls for a small amount of chili powder and a bay leaf.

The fifth edition of *Joy of Cooking* (1964) contains a recipe that calls for onion or garlic, chili powder and a bay leaf (pp 430). By contrast, the recipe in the eighth edition of *Joy* (2006) calls for TEN cloves of garlic and one fourth CUP of chili powder (pp 513).

The first documented record of chili being eaten was in the 1820s in San Antonio, Texas. Food historians believe it is an American invention — it didn't come from Mexico — and it was a recipe that rose from humble roots. Originally it was just beef cooked with chilis. It was prepared by chuck wagon cooks, prospectors, Army cooks, and cooks in Texas prisons.

As time went on, other ingredients found their way into popular recipes for the dish. Wayne Preston Allen gives a concise description on his Web site, quoting a 1990 article in Chile Pepper Magazine by John Thorn:

"The first Army publication to give a recipe for chili was published in 1896, The Manual for Army Cooks (War Department Document #18). By World War I, the Army had added garlic and beans; by World War II, tomatoes. This was a national pattern: Fannie Farmer did exactly the same (see the editions for 1914, 1930, and 1941)."[26]

By the late 1800s the recipe had spread out of the southwest. In the 1920s, "chili parlors" sprang up in many places and remained popular, off and on, until they were replaced by chain hamburger restaurants in the 1950s.

Dan Wall's Chili House in Harlem was the fabled site of legendary jazz saxophonist Charlie Parker's 1939 epiphany that led to his complex, influential style.[27]

Chili powder (a spice blend of dried, ground chilis, cumin, oregano, garlic powder and salt), first created in Texas in the 1890s, became available across the U.S. by the early 20th century.

Chili has become one of the country's favorite dishes and by 1980, canned chili (first sold in the early 1900s) was one of the best-selling canned foods in the U.S.[28]

Chili con carne was a staple in Joan's kitchen. Linda remembers:

"My mother always made it with rice. There'd be a pot of chili and a pot of rice on the stove and everybody would help themselves. They all came in at different times."

Ingredients:

1 cup onions, diced finely
2 stalks celery (about 1 cup), diced finely
1 green pepper, diced finely (about 1 cup)
1/2 cup parsley, finely chopped
1 tbsp Crisco (or olive oil)
2 pounds ground beef
2 15.5 oz cans dark red kidney beans
1 quart of tomatoes
1/4 cup catsup
1 tsp salt
pepper

Directions:

Heat the Crisco in a large pan or Dutch oven, then add the vegetables and stir until they soften and begin to brown, about five minutes.

Add the ground beef and break it up as it cooks. Brown it slightly, about five minutes.

Add the kidney beans, tomatoes, catsup, salt and pepper.

Simmer 5-10 minutes.

Joan's Greek Chili used in Cincinnati 5-way chili (with spaghetti, beans, onion and cheese)

Greek Chili

(Notebook 2, pp 41)

This is a unique recipe. It would be intriguing to think that it was "the" recipe for the famous Cincinnati Chili first created in the 1920s, but we have no information at all about its origin.

We don't know if Joan ever made it. We suspect she might have gotten it from one of the Greek diner owners she worked for. Since Greek restaurant owners famously have huge extended family networks of cousins (who all own restaurants or diners) it wouldn't be out of the realm of possibility that this recipe made its way east from Cincinnati. Or, Joan picked it out of a magazine. Or, Joan picked it out of a magazine and tweaked it.

Wherever it came from, it is surely **descended** from one of those recipes which are now a famous regional dish in the Cincinnati area, most notably served with spaghetti and cheese (three way): spaghetti, onion and cheese (four way) or spaghetti, cheese, onion and beans (five way).

This isn't really "chili," which was a dish of meat and peppers from the American southwest (see "Chili Con Carne"). It's really a meat sauce create with seasonings common in the Balkan countries and was served over hot dogs as well as on spaghetti.

The original "Empress" chili was created in Cincinnati by Tom and John Kiradjieff, immigrants from Slavic Macedonia, who served it at their small restaurant located next to the Empress burlesque theatre. The seasonings are typical of Balkan cooking and there is a vaguely similar dish of Greek origin — a meat sauce called saltsa kima that is served over spaghetti.

By the 1940s Greek immigrant Nicholas Lambrinides copied the dish and began serving "Skyline Chili" in his Skyline Diner in Cincinnati. The Empress and Skyline establishments went on to become restaurant chains and their chili is available canned and frozen. Many other restaurants in the Cincinnati area have also begun serving their versions and it has become an iconic regional American dish.[29]

A recipe for it first showed up in the seventh edition of *Joy of Cooking* (1997) under the name "Cincinnati Chili Cockaigne."

John Becker, great grandson of the original *Joy* author Irma Starkloff Rombauer, wrote on the *Joy* Web site that the recipe was one that his father Ethan Becker had created more than 20 years ago for a Cincinnati chili cook off (he won). He said Ethan had gotten some hints about the Kiradjieffs seasonings from a childhood friend of one of the Kiradjieff's sons.[30]

I have been making Cincinnati five-way chili since the 1980s after hearing of it from a Cincinnati native who described the "way" system and said "just make your normal chili with no beans and put some cinnamon in it."

It has been a family favorite for many years and we were very happy to find this more authentic version that Joan had recorded.

Ingredients:
4 cups water
2 pounds lean ground beef
2 cups chopped onion
2 15-oz cans tomato sauce

4 cloves garlic

3 tbsp chili powder

2 tsp cinnamon

1 1/2 tsp salt

1 to 1 1/2 tbsp allspice

1 tsp cumin

1/2 tsp red pepper

2 bay leaves

2 tbsp white vinegar

2 tbsp Worcestershire sauce

Directions:

Bring the water to a boil, add the ground beef and simmer 30 minutes. Skim off the fat and discard it.

Add remaining ingredients and simmer two hours.

Discard bay leaves

This can be eaten immediately, but it does benefit from sitting overnight.

Hamburger gravy over mashed potatoes

This was a very popular dinner dish in the 1950s and 60s. It was cheap and easy and kids ate it. Joan had no recipe for it but Linda and I both remember it well. I also remember the smell of it cooking in my grandmother's kitchen.

Ingredients:
(mashed potatoes)
1 1/2 pounds potatoes, peeled and sliced in 1/4-inch slices
2 tbsp butter
1/4 cup milk
1/2 tsp salt
1/4 tsp pepper
(gravy)
2 tbsp butter
1 cup coarsely chopped onions
1 pound ground beef (I used Angus)
2 cups beef stock
3 tbsp flour
1/2 tsp salt
1/4 tsp pepper

Directions:

(start potatoes)

Put potatoes in water to cover in a sauce pan, bring to boil and cook at a slow boil for 15 minutes.

(hamburger gravy)

Melt butter in a frying pan and sauté onions until they are soft, about 4 minutes. Add the hamburger and sauté until it is just brown, four or five minutes.

Stir in the salt, pepper and flour and mix well. Add the beef stock, bring to a boil and cook, stirring, until it thickens slightly, three to four minutes.

Cover and allow to sit on low heat.

(finish mashed potatoes)

Drain the potatoes and mash with a hand masher. Place in mixer bowl with the butter, milk, salt and pepper and mix well.

To serve, place mashed potatoes in a flattened pile on a plate and top with hamburger gravy.

(serves four)

Cheesy Stroganoff

(Notebook 2, pp 27)

Ingredients:

2 strips bacon

2 tbsp butter

2 pounds top round roast, chipped

2 cups onion, chopped coarsely
3 cloves garlic, minced
1/2 cup flour
1 cup red wine
4 cups beef stock
2 cups mushrooms, chopped coarsely
1/2 cup red onion, chopped coarsely
1/2 cup scallions, sliced coarsely
Sour cream
1 pound medium egg noodles.

Directions:
Render the bacon in a Dutch oven over medium heat for about five minutes. Add the butter and brown the beef – perhaps two minutes. Add the onion and garlic and sauté until onions are clear, then add the flour and mix well.

Add the wine and beef stock, stir well and bring to boil.

Add the mushrooms, red onion and scallions. Stir in one cup sour cream, cover with two cups cheddar cheese and bake in a 350-degree oven until the cheese melts and is bubbly, about 30 minutes.

Serve over medium egg noodles with a dollop of sour cream on top.

Veal Paprika Rice

(Notebook 1 page 31)

Ingredients:

3 tbsp flour

1 tsp salt

1/2 tsp pepper

3/4 pound veal, sliced thinly in two by one inch strips

3/4 cup thinly sliced onions

4 tbsp butter

2 tsp paprika

12 oz (1 can) evaporated milk

Directions:

Mix the flour, salt and pepper and dredge the veal strips in it.

Melt the butter in a frying pan and sauté the onions until they are golden brown. Add the veal and continue sautéing for about five minutes, or until they are browned slightly.

Add the paprika and mix well. Add the milk and stir constantly until it thickens. Simmer for two or three minutes.

Serve over rice.

Casseroles

Spaghetti Pizza Style

(Notebook 2, pp 48)

This is an interesting recipe. It almost appears to be a variation on Jewish noodle kugel — noodles baked with milk and egg (and other things).

Linda's brother Tom Scheetz said he remembered finding the recipe in a *Highlights* children's magazine when he was in grade school and gave it to Joan.

We also found a recipe that was cut from a box of Creamette spaghetti (below). In Joan's recipe, everything is doubled except the milk and eggs. Possibly the recipe that she used could have been the one from the children's magazine. That, of course, would make it more filling for a house full of hungry eaters.

According to the brand web site, Creamette pasta was first branded in 1912:

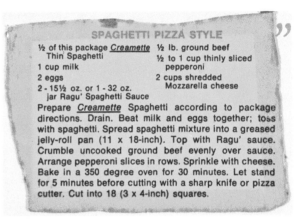

A loan of $100 is all it took for James T. Williams to open a grocery store in Minneapolis in 1896. But this businessman's legacy would not be in the goods he sold but the product he developed in 1912. Williams redesigned elbow macaroni with a thinner wall and larger hole and, as a result, invented the first quick-cooking pasta.

SPAGHETTI PIZZA STYLE

½ of this package *Creamette* Thin Spaghetti
1 cup milk
2 eggs
2 - 15½ oz. or 1 - 32 oz. jar Ragu' Spaghetti Sauce

½ lb. ground beef
½ to 1 cup thinly sliced pepperoni
2 cups shredded Mozzarella cheese

Prepare *Creamette* Spaghetti according to package directions. Drain. Beat milk and eggs together; toss with spaghetti. Spread spaghetti mixture into a greased jelly-roll pan (11 x 18-inch). Top with Ragu' sauce. Crumble uncooked ground beef evenly over sauce. Arrange pepperoni slices in rows. Sprinkle with cheese. Bake in a 350 degree oven for 30 minutes. Let stand for 5 minutes before cutting with a sharp knife or pizza cutter. Cut into 18 (3 x 4-inch) squares.

Williams named his macaroni Creamette®. The Minnesota Macaroni Company manufactured the Creamette® brand until Williams bought out the firm and Creamette® became its official new name. The history of innovation that Williams employed to create his fast-cooking noodles was indicative of the spirit that propelled Creamette® to a leading share position throughout much of the Midwest.

In the 1950s, consumers came to know Creamette® as the "recipe company" for the easy recipes listed on every box. Creamette® has grown from a regional brand popular across the Midwest to a regional favorite. It's widely distributed in 37 states through the U.S. Creamette® was run by the Williams family until 1979 when it was sold to the Borden Dairy Company®.[31]

It was a very popular recipe in the Scheetz household. Linda and Ken Jr. remember it fondly. According to Linda, Joan always used Spatini spaghetti sauce mix to make it.

Spatini makes more than just a great-tasting spaghetti sauce - It's a delicious blend of all-natural Italian herbs and spices that can perfectly season a variety of dishes. Use it to perk up fried chicken, meat loaf, fish fillets - even a homemade soup! So, treat your family to some tasty new recipe ideas - all with a little help from Spatini. Any way you use it - Spatini is delicious. Buon Appetito!

The dry season packets were sold by the Spatini company of Englewood Cliffs, N.J., from 1952 until the company was purchased by Lipton in the early 1970s. Lipton sold the mix to consumers until 2007. Since then it has been available only for restaurant and institutional use.[32] Wal-Mart's Web site sells an institutional size: 12 15-oz packets to make 2.5 gallons of sauce each. It is sold under the Lawry label.

There is a recipe for it on the Web[33] which is largely oregano, thyme, sugar, cornstarch, garlic and onion.

Preheat oven to: 350 degrees

Ingredients:
1/2 pound spaghetti
1/2 cup milk
1 egg
16 oz. tomato sauce
1/2 pound ground beef
1/4 pound pepperoni sliced thinly
3/4 pound grated mozzarella or provolone cheese

Directions:

Cook spaghetti, drain, place in greased eight-by-eight-inch baking dish.
Beat egg and milk and pour over spaghetti.
Cover evenly with tomato sauce.
Distribute the RAW ground beef evenly over top.
Cover with pepperoni slices then grated cheese.
Bake 350 degrees for 30 minutes. Let stand five to 10 minutes before serving.

Beef Corn Casserole

(Notebook 1, pp 39, Notebook 2 pp 28)

This recipe was believed lost by most family members and its rediscovery was met with great joy, especially by Ken, Jr. It's one of those simple casseroles intended to fill hungry kids' stomachs, but it's rather interesting. Joan's recipe calls for ground beef, but to improve it you can use sirloin ground in the food processor.

Preheat oven to: 350 degrees
Baking dish: 8 by 8 inches

Ingredients
1 cup bread crumbs
2 tsp mustard
1 tsp thyme
1 1/2 tsp salt

2 eggs
1/4 cup milk
1 tsp Worcestershire sauce
2 1/2 cups creamed corn
1/4 cup finely chopped onion
1 1/2 pounds ground beef

Directions
Combine the bread crumbs, mustard, thyme and salt and set aside

Combine the eggs, milk, Worcestershire sauce, corn and onion in large mixing bowl. Add the beef and mix well. Add the bread crumbs and dry ingredients and mix well.

Turn into greased two-quart eight-by-eight-inch baking dish.

Bake 350 degrees for 1 hour.

Chicken 'N Biscuits

(Notebook 2, pp 15)

Preheat oven to: 400 degrees
Baking dish: 8 by 10

Ingredients:
(Casserole)
8 slices bacon, fried crisp and crumbled
2 1/2 cups cooked chicken or turkey, cubed
1 10-oz package frozen mixed vegetables, cooked and drained
OR one cup mushrooms OR one cup diced tomatoes
1 1/2 cup shredded cheddar or yellow American cheese
1 can cream of chicken soup (or Béchamel sauce substitute, see "Sauces" chapter)
3/4 cup milk

(Biscuits)
2 cups flour
2 tsp baking powder
1/2 tsp baking soda
1 tsp salt
1 tbsp sugar
1/3 cup butter
1 cup milk or buttermilk
1/2 can (1.4 oz) French fried onions

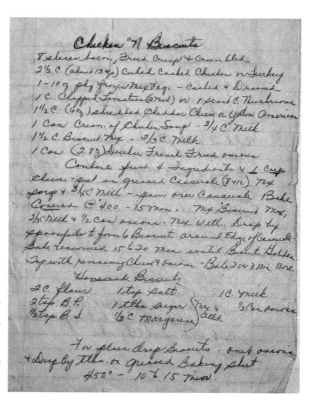

Directions:
(Casserole)
Combine the bacon, chicken, vegetables and one cup of the cheese and pour into greased eight-by-10 inch casserole.

Mix soup and milk and pour over the other ingredients.

Bake, covered, at 400 degrees for 15 minutes.

(Biscuits)
Combine the dry ingredients, cut in the butter then stir in the milk and half the fried onions.

Drop by spoonful on top of casserole OR, roll out and cut with biscuit cutter and place on top of casserole and bake uncovered 15-20 minutes or until biscuits are golden brown. Top with remaining cheese (1/2 cup) and remaining onions and bake two or three minutes.

Zucchini Casserole

(Notebook 2, pp 46)

Preheat oven to: 350 degrees
Baking dish: 9 by 13 inch

Ingredients:
3 small zucchini squash, sliced thinly (1/4 inch)
1 qt tomatoes, chopped
3/4 cup onion, coarsely chopped
1 small green or red pepper, chopped
1 large clove garlic
olive oil
2 tsp salt
2 tbsp sugar
1/2 tsp thyme
1/2 tsp basil

8 oz Rigatoni
9 slices of American cheese
16 oz Mozzarella cheese, grated
1 cup grated Parmesan cheese

Directions:
Sauté squash, tomato, onion and pepper in olive oil until soft, 10 minutes. Add garlic, salt, sugar, thyme and basil.

Cook rigatoni according to directions on box, about 10 minutes.

Pour vegetable mixture into greased nine-by-13-inch casserole then top with pasta. Cover the pasta with the American cheese, then the mozzarella, then the Parmesan.

Cover with aluminum foil and bake in 350-degree oven for 45 minutes, or until bubbly. Remove foil last 10 minutes.

Yolanda's Lasagna

(Cards #2 and #4: Notebook 2 pp 49)

Lin and her brothers all remember this recipe and Linda remembers Yolanda Beaty. She was a friend of Joan's in the late 1960s or early 70s, slender with brown hair and brown eyes. She lived in an apartment in Quakertown and had a little boy named Rusty. Linda remembered that he had freckles. Yolanda's apartment had a living room on the third floor, which fascinated Linda.

The recipe card from Joan's recipe box (#2) features a strange spelling: "Lazanne" which might have been from Yolanda. Joan spelled it correctly when she copied the recipe onto a card that was her recipe box #4.

Preheat oven to: 350 degrees
Baking dish: 9-by-13 inch

Ingredients:
1 pound lasagna noodles
1 32 oz recipe spaghetti sauce (see "sauces")
1 pound ground beef
16 oz grated mozzarella cheese
16 oz ricotta cheese
salt

Directions:
Cook the lasagna noodles according to package directions.
Make the sauce or bring 32 oz of sauce to a boil.
Sauté the ground beef until it is cooked.
In a 9-by-13 inch baking dish assemble the lasagna as follows:

— enough tomato sauce to cover the bottom
— cover with four noodles
— half the ground beef and half the tomato sauce
— four noodles
— half the ricotta and 1/3 of the mozzarella
— four noodles
— the remaining half of the ground beef and remaining half of the tomato sauce
— four noodles
— the remaining half of the ricotta and 1/3 of the mozzarella
— four noodles
— the remaining 1/3 of the mozzarella

Cover with aluminum foil and bake 30 minutes at 350 degrees. Allow to cool 10 minutes before serving.

Lasagna Spinach Rollups

(Notebook 2, pp 37)

Preheat oven to: 350 degrees
Baking dish: 8-by-11 inch

Ingredients:
16 oz. ricotta cheese
2 boxes spinach thawed and with most of the water squeezed out
1 1/2 cups mozzarella cheese

2 eggs
1/2 cup parmesan cheese
1 tsp basil
Salt and pepper to taste

1 box lasagna noodles, cooked minimum time
2 quarts tomato sauce (heated)

Directions:

Put the ricotta, spinach, mozzarella, eggs, parmesan cheese, basil, salt and pepper in a bowl and combine well.

Cook the lasagna noodles the minimum time. Drain the noodles in a colander and spray with cold water to cool them enough to handle.

Spread a little tomato sauce in the bottom of an eight-by-11-inch baking pan.

Spread out one of the lasagna noodles on a cutting board and spread with the filling. Roll up and place on its side in the baking dish. Continue until all noodles are used up.

To estimate how much filling you will need for each noodle, smooth the filling in the mixing bowl and using a knife to draw an "X" across the top, dividing the bowl into fourths. Since there are 20 lasagna noodles in a box, use one fifth of the filling from each quarter of the bowl for each rollup.

When all the noodles have been filled and are in the baking dish, pour the tomato sauce over them and sprinkle with parmesan then mozzarella cheese.

Bake, uncovered, 45-55 minutes or until hot in the center.

Chicken Divan

(Notebook 1, pp 4)

Chicken Divan was popular throughout Joan's life time and there are numerous recipes for it on the Web today.

The earliest Chicken Divan recipe we found in The *New York Times* was in the *Times* magazine of January 18, 1948 (pp 28), in a food feature "The Chicken in the Pot." Writer Jane Nickerson attributed it to the Divan Parisien restaurant at 17 East 45th St. in New York City. The recipe calls for cooking a stewing hen for three hours, mixing the meat with broccoli, covering it with a mix of sauces and a lot of Parmesan cheese then browning it under the broiler.

In the January 17, 1964, edition (pp 20), in a "Directory to Dining," the *Times* wrote:

> "*Divan Parisien, 33 East 48th Street, EL 5-6726. A popular restaurant that is reputedly the point of origin for chicken Divan. The menu of the establishment is nondescript and, broadly speaking, so is the food.*

Poppy Cannon had a quick-and-easy but not very appealing recipe in her 1952 *Can Opener Cookbook* (pp 118) made with broccoli or asparagus, sliced deli chicken, egg white, mayonnaise and grated cheese heated for 10 minutes.

The May, 1950, issue of *Better Homes and Gardens* had an add-a-can-of-soup recipe (pp 196) for an asparagus recipe that was called Chicken Divan. It looks suspiciously like a convenience food version of the Divan Parisien recipe and perhaps the ancestor of the super-fast Poppy Cannon creation.

The Fifth edition of *Joy of Cooking* in 1964 (pp 236) had a recipe that called for toast slices topped with sliced chicken covered with cooked broccoli, Mornay sauce and parmesan cheese.

The Great Radio Ask Your Neighbor Cookbook, the 1974 community cookbook printed in Pottsville, Pa., contains a recipe very similar to Joan and Linda's (minus the rice) contributed by Theresa Toth of Nesquehoning.

Joan obviously got this recipe from Linda since "(Linda)" is written on the upper right of the notebook entry. The rice in this recipe makes it different from the traditional dish. The use of heavy cream also makes it stand apart from the "fast-and-easy" versions that call for canned soup.

Preheat oven to: 350 degrees
Baking pan: three-quart baking dish or casserole

Ingredients
(casserole)
1 cup rice, cooked and drained
1 pound broccoli, stems peeled and cut in 1/2-inch pieces, florets broken into one-inch pieces then steamed until barely soft.
3 large chicken breasts, cut in 1 1/2-inch cubes and simmered in one cup chicken stock until just cooked.

(sauce)
1 cup heavy cream

1 cup chicken stock (use the stock the chicken was cooked in, adding water to bring it to one cup if necessary)

3 tbsp flour

2 tbsp butter

1/4 cup parmesan cheese

Directions:

(sauce)

Melt butter in sauce pan, add the flour and make a roux. Stir in the chicken stock from the cooked chicken and stir until thickened. Remove from heat and cool the pan a few minutes then stir in the cream.

(assembly)

Put hot rice in three-quart baking dish and top with broccoli. Add salt and pepper to taste. Pour one half of the sauce over it. Top with the chicken pieces.

Mix the parmesan cheese with the remaining half of the sauce and pour over the chicken. Sprinkle more parmesan cheese over top.

Bake in a 350-degree oven for 25 minutes.

Beenie Weenie Casserole

(Cards #3)

Joan commonly used a corn-bread mix but we give directions below for making corn bread from scratch.

Preheat oven to: 350 degrees
Baking dish: 8-by-8-inch

Ingredients:
1/2 pound hot dogs cut in one-inch pieces
2 tbsp olive oil

1/2 cup onion, chopped coarsely

2 cans baked beans, drained, with the liquid reserved
1/4 cup barbecue sauce
3 tbsp brown sugar

(corn bread topping)
1/2 cup corn meal
1/3 cup plus one tbsp flour
2 tbsp sugar
1 1/4 tsp baking powder
1/4 tsp salt
1/2 cup milk
1 egg, beaten
3 tbsp melted butter or baking drippings

Directions:

Heat olive oil in large frying pan and brown the hot dogs on all sides, about five minutes. Add onions and sauté until translucent, about three minutes.

Add the beans, barbecue sauce and sugar to the pan along with one half cup of the reserved juice from the beans. Stir to combine and bring to boil. Reduce heat to simmer while you make the corn bread topping.

Make corn bread topping by mixing the dry ingredients in one bowl and the wet ingredients in another. Combine the two and stir until well mixed.

Pour the hot dog-bean mixture into a greased 8-by-8 inch casserole. Pour the cornbread topping on top and use a spatula to spread it evenly across the top.

Bake 30 minutes.

Skillet Tamale Pie

(Notebooks 2, pp 17, and 3, pp 9)

There are LOTS of recipes for "skillet tamale pie." Most are chili made in a frying pan, topped with cornbread then baked in the oven. Joan found one she considered "* excellent" (see photo of her recipe). She must have liked it because she had identical copies of the recipe in two different notebooks. A Google search turned up the recipe, dated 2011 in the *Women's Day* magazine. Joan cut down the amount of creamed corn in the topping, increased the tomato sauce in the chili and increased the amount of chili powder.

Cooking pan: Dutch oven

Ingredients:
(chili)
3/4 pound, (12 oz) ground beef
3/4 cup chopped scallions
1 3/4 cups tomato sauce
1 15-oz can black beans (rinsed)
1 tbsp chili powder
1 tsp cumin
3/4 cup water

(topping)
1/4 cup milk
1 egg, beaten
1 cup creamed corn
4 1/2 oz chopped green chilis (two large jalapeño peppers)
1/4 cup chopped scallions
1 8 1/2 oz box cornmeal muffin mix

Directions:
(Chili)
In a Dutch oven, cook the ground beef and scallions until the meat is cooked. Add the tomato sauce, black beans, chili powder, cumin and water. Simmer for 15 minutes.

(Topping)
Combine the milk, egg, creamed corn, chilis and one fourth cup scallions. Mix in the muffin mix.
Bring the chili to a boil then turn off the heat. CAREFULLY, spoon the topping on the chili, taking care to spread it evenly across the surface. It will be quite liquid. Put the lid on the pan and turn the burner to simmer for 15 minutes. The top should be slightly dry and a toothpick inserted should come out with just a few crumbs on it.

Ravoli Lasagne

(Cards #3)

Preheat oven to: 375 degrees
Baking dish: 8-by-8-inch

Ingredients:

2 15-oz cans beef ravioli

2 cups diced tomatoes, drained well

1 1/2 tsp Italian seasoning

1 cup chopped spinach (if frozen, bring to room temperature an squeeze out most of the water)

1 cup small-curd cottage cheese (or Ricotta)

1/2 tsp black pepper

1 cup Mozzarella cheese, grated

Directions:

Mix the ravioli, tomatoes and Italian seasoning in a bowl. Heat in microwave

Mix the spinach, cottage cheese (or Ricotta) and pepper.

Grease the eight-by-eight baking dish and put in half the ravioli mixture, topped with half the spinach-cheese mixture then top with half the mozzarella cheese.

Cover that with the other half of the ravioli mixture, then the other half of the spinach-cheese mixture and the other half of the mozzarella.

Bake at 375 degrees for 30-40 minutes.

Meat and Sausage

Meatloaf

(Notebook 1, pp 41)

Joan's recipe contains a note with a date for this one: "Best of all 2002."

Linda remembers it well and with good reason. it is a very good meat loaf — moist, with just enough substance to hold together.

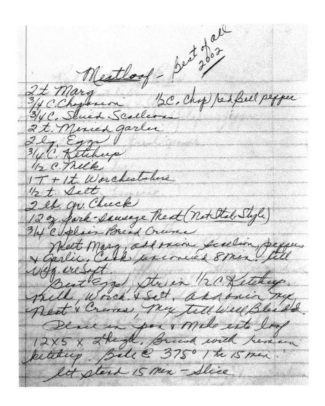

Preheat oven to: 375 degrees

Baking pan: baking sheet

Ingredients:

2 tbsp olive oil

3/4 cup onion, chopped finely

3/4 cup scallions, sliced thinly

1/2 cup sweet red pepper, chopped finely

2 tsp garlic, chopped finely

2 eggs

1/2 cup catsup

1/2 cup milk

1 tbsp plus one tsp Worcestershire sauce

1/2 tsp salt

2 pounds lean ground beef

12 oz loose pork sausage

3/4 cup bread crumbs

(topping)

1/4 cup catsup

Directions:

Sauté the onions, scallions, peppers and garlic in the olive oil until soft — about eight minutes.

In a mixing bowl, beat the eggs then stir in 1/2 cup catsup, the milk, Worcestershire sauce and salt. Mix well then add the reserved onion-pepper-garlic mixture, meat and crumbs. Combine well.

Place on baking pan or baking sheet and form into a long loaf. Brush with 1/4 cup catsup and bake at 375 degrees for one hour and 15 minutes.

Remove from oven and allow to cool for 15 minutes before serving.

Ham Loaf

(Notebook 1, pp 12 and Cards #1)

Linda remembered ham loaf very well:

" *Ham loaf was one of my favorite things when I was a kid. I always asked for it for my birthday with potato filling and John Cope's Dried Corn. After holidays my mother would save the leftover dried corn and keep it in a container in the back of the frig and I'd eat it.* "

Linda has been making this for years. It might be her signature dish. Her "famous ham loaf dinner" always includes a very large ham loaf, mashed potatoes and corn.

This isn't a delicate recipe. It can linger in the oven for half an hour or more while guests wander in.

We found what appears to be the original recipe in recipe box #1, with the note "Winnie Scheetz."

Preheat oven to: 350 degrees
Baking pan: baking sheet

Ingredients:
1 pound smoked ham, ground
2 pounds beef, pork, veal meatloaf blend
1 cup bread crumbs
3 eggs, beaten
1 1/2 cups milk
salt to taste
One can of condensed tomato soup

Directions:
Mix all ingredients (except the tomato soup) well. Form into long meat loaf in a greased pan or baking sheet.

Spread the condensed tomato soup over the top.

Bake at 350 degrees for 1 1/2 hours.

Salisbury Steak

(Notebook 1, pp 44 and Notebook 11, pp 41)
Preheat oven to: 350 degrees
Baking dish: 9-by-13 inches

Ingredients:
(patties)
1 1/2 pounds beef, chopped in food processor
1/2 tsp dill

1/2 tsp oregano

1 tsp parsley flakes

1 clove garlic, minced

3/4 cups milk

1/2 cup bread crumbs

1/2 cup oatmeal

1 tbsp onion, minced

1 tsp salt

1/2 tsp pepper

(sauce)

4 cups onion-beef gravy

Directions:

Mix all ingredients well and shape into six patties. Put in casserole and bake at 350 degrees for 20 minutes

Pour gravy over patties and bake for an additional 50 minutes.

To make onion-beef gravy:

Ingredients:

1 cup onions chopped finely

6 tbsp butter

1 tbsp olive oil

6 tbsp flour

1/2 tsp salt

4 cup beef stock

Directions:

Carmelize the onions in the butter and olive oil. Use a medium to medium-low heat so they don't burn. This will probably take about 20 minutes.

When the onions are brown, add the flour and salt and stir to mix thoroughly. Add the beef stock and bring to a boil, stirring, to thicken.

BAR-B-QUE BEEF

1 (2-3 lb.) chuck roast   1 tsp. chili powder
2 onions, chopped   3/4 tsp. pepper
3/4 c. catsup   2 Tbsp. brown sugar
3/4 c. water   1 Tbsp. vinegar
1 tsp. salt   1 Tbsp. Worcestershire
1 tsp. paprika   sauce
1 tsp. garlic salt

     Simmer together all day. Serve on rolls.
Serves 6-8.
                 Jean Rudolph

Hamburger Bar-B-Que

(*Corps* Cookbook, pp 37)

This recipe came from the *Corps* cookbook. It's one of those popular American dishes that show up whenever a lot of people are to be fed. We have a 14-inch cast iron frying pan that Joan gave Linda many years ago. Linda's grandmother Florence always used it to make large quantities of this barbecue. We always use that pan to make the "Bar-B-Que" and it's in the accompanying picture.

Like many highly seasoned dishes, if you prepare this the day before it is to be served the flavors are really heightened. It's not a delicate concoction and it can sit on the stove (or in a chafing dish) on a low heat for hours.

Ingredients:

2-3 pounds lean hamburger or lean beef ground in food processor
2 large onions
3/4 cup catsup
3/4 cup water
1 tsp salt
1 tsp paprika
1 large clove garlic, chopped finely
1 tsp chili powder
3/4 tsp pepper
2 tbsp brown sugar
1 tbsp vinegar
1 tbsp Worcestershire sauce

Directions:

Combine all ingredients, simmer 30 minutes (or more) then make sandwiches on hamburger rolls. Can be kept warm in crock pot.

Pork and sauerkraut

Pork is the Pennsylvania Dutch "good luck" dish on New Year's Day. And roast pork in that world is usually accompanied by sauerkraut and mashed or roasted potatoes. In Joan's world, pork and sauerkraut were eaten other times of the year as well. Actually, it was eaten often. Joan roasted pork in a slow cooker with sauerkraut and onions.

Ingredients:
1 two or three pound pork loin
1 quart of sauerkraut
1 large onion, cut in 16ths.

Directions:
Put the sauerkraut and onions in a slow cooker, put the pork roast on top and cook on medium heat for five or six hours. It can be turned to low and allowed to sit while guests arrive or other delays are dealt with.

Serve with mashed potatoes, buweschenkel, potato filling or roast potatoes.

Serves 4-6.

Hog Maw (stuffed pig stomach)

Hog maw, or stuffed pig stomach, is a major conversation starter. There is definitely a "yuck" factor for many people, especially kids. However, that usually fades into the background when they realize they don't have to eat the stomach part. The rest is pretty ordinary, largely potatoes and pork sausage.

Joan made it least once, Linda remembered, but she had no recipe for it. It's a popular dish throughout south central and south eastern Pennsylvania. In Cumberland County here in south central Pennsylvania we see rural churches advertising hog maw dinners from time to time. Two waitresses in the Cocoa Diner in Hershey (Lebanon County) told me they made it, though not often, and shared their recipes with me. One said it was her grandmother's recipe. The mother of one of Linda's friends, who lives in northern York County, makes it — filled with cabbage and sausage — about once every month.

Alan Tumblin, operator of the Castlerigg wine bar in Carlisle, who moved to Lancaster County from Ohio many years ago, had never heard of it. His Amish employer, with typical Amish wit, told him about it and said that locally it was called "Amish goose."

Fresh, cleaned pig stomachs are available in butcher shops in the Carlisle area. The Karns Foods markets in the county regularly stock them frozen.

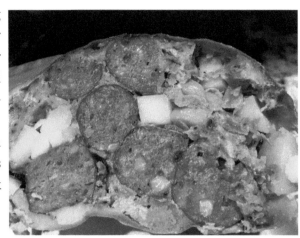

There were six recipes for "pig stomach" in the charity cookbooks that Joan owned:

— *Boyertown Cookery*, pp 13
— *Heirloom Cookbook*, pp 43: (called "Hog Maul")
— *Schwenkfelder Cook Book*. pp 91

To assemble one, rinse the stomach, then turn it inside out and sew up the smaller two openings with a darning needle and kitchen string. Turn it right-side-out, fill it with about 12 cups of filling and sew up the larger opening. The filled stomach then can be either steamed or roasted for four hours. Recipes usually call for the the steamed version to be browned in butter in a frying pan after it's cooked.

Common fillings include various combinations of:
— Potatoes
— Onions
— Carrots
— Celery
— Green peppers
— Cabbage
— Smoked sausage (cut in small pieces)
— Loose sausage
— Spare ribs

The filling combinations almost always include potatoes, onions and some form of pork. The choice of vegetables varies widely. One style substitutes cabbage for the potatoes.

To serve, cut the finished maw in one and one-half inch slices. Eating the actual stomach is optional.

Ingredients:
1 cleaned pig stomach
4 cups peeled potatoes cut in 1/2-inch dice
1 large stalk celery cut in 1/2-inch slices
1 large onion chopped coarsely
1 1/2 pounds loose sausage
1 1/2 pounds smoked sausage cut in 1-inch slices
2 tsp marjoram
1 tsp salt
pepper
olive oil

Directions:
Turn the stomach inside out, sew up the small openings then turn it right side out.
Mix all other ingredients (except olive oil) in a mixing bowl then stuff it all in the stomach.
Sew up the large opening.
Brush with olive oil, place on rack in roasting pan and roast at 350 degrees for four hours. Turn after three hours to brown it evenly.
It is commonly served with gravy.

Corn Flake Encrusted Hot Dogs

There was no recipe for this. Linda remembered Joan making them not infrequently in the 1970s. They are clearly kid pleasers since they're made of hot dogs and breakfast cereal.

Preheat oven to: 350

Ingredients:
4 hot dogs
1 cup corn flakes, crushed
1/2 cup catsup

Directions:
Spread the catsup on a plate and the corn flakes on another plate. Roll the hot dogs in the catsup to coat them thoroughly then roll in the corn flakes.
Place on greased baking sheet.
Bake 350 degrees for 20 minutes.

Pot Roast

In Joan's world, pot roast was a staple. Like many U.S. moms in her age, she cooked chuck steak in a large pot on top of the stove in liquid flavored with an instant onion soup mix. That onion-roasting-beef aroma still wafts over the streets of small towns in warm weather when the windows are open an hour or so before "supper time."

Joan left no recipe, however, Linda remembers in detail how she made it. Joan used cheaper, fatty cuts of beef and Linda, who hated fat in even tiny amounts, usually ate the vegetables, potatoes and juice with just enough meat to stay out of trouble. According to Linda, it MUST be browned in vegetable shortening.

Linda prefers leaner meat and insists that an eye of round is the only acceptable cut of beef to use.

Ingredients:
3 pound eye of round
2 tbsp flour
salt
pepper
3 tbsp vegetable shortening
3 cups water

3 medium potatoes cut in quarters

3 carrots, scrubbed and cut in half lengthwise then in three-inch lengths

2 medium onions, peeled and cut in quarters

1 package dry onion soup mix

Directions:

Mix the flour with the salt and pepper then coat the beef with it. Melt the shortening in a Dutch oven and brown the meat on all sides.

Add the water, bring to a boil and simmer for one hour.

Add the vegetables and onion soup mix and simmer, covered for an additional hour.

Sausage I (pork)

(Notebook 1, pp 19)

This is an incredibly simple way to make sausage. The alternative is press it into patties and fry it. Rolling it in aluminum foil and simmering it until it's done also is a slightly low-fat method of preparing sausage, which by the way is usually one third fat and two third lean meat.

The water that it simmers in also makes a nice soup stock, which can be frozen if there is no immediate need for it.

Ingredients:

2 pounds ground meat (loose pork sausage works nicely and a blend of 3/4 pork sausage and 1/4 ground beef is an interesting combination).

1 tsp salt

1/2 tsp pepper

1 tbsp fresh garlic chopped finely

1 tbsp fennel seed ground fine in a mortar and pestle

2 tbsp sun dried tomatoes in olive oil, chopped finely

1/2 cup water

Directions:

Mix the ingredients all together. Put one fourth of the mixture on each of four 12-by-12-inch pieces of aluminum foil.

Form into a long mound of sausage to within one inch of the end of the foil.

Roll up the foil, making a round sausage. Crimp the ends tightly.

Put in a 12-inch or, if you have one, a 14-inch frying pan and pour on three cups of water. Cover and bring to a boil. Reduce the heat and simmer for 20 minutes.

Sausage II (beef)

(Cards #1)

I've made a minor change to this one. I substituted fresh garlic for garlic powder because I simply have an aversion to dehydrated garlic. I also left out the Nature's seasoning since its main ingredient is salt and the other ingredients are dried parsley, dried garlic and dried onion.

Ingredients:
2 pounds lean ground beef
2 tbsp pickling salt
3 tbsp coarsely ground pepper
3 tbsp mustard seed
1 tsp fresh garlic, shopped finely
1 tbsp onion, chopped finely
1 tsp parsley
1 cup water

Directions:
Mix the ingredients all together. Put one third of the mixture on each of three 12-by-12-inch pieces of aluminum foil.

Form into a long mound of sausage to within one inch of the ends of the foil.

Roll up the foil, making a round sausage. Crimp the ends tightly.

Place in refrigerator for 24 hours.

Put in a 12-inch frying pan and pour on three cups of water. Cover and bring to a boil. Reduce the heat and simmer for 20 minutes.

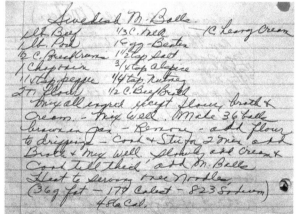

Swedish Meatballs

(Notebook 1, pp 8)

Ingredients:
(meat balls)
1 pound lean ground beef
1 pound ground pork
1/2 cup bread crumbs
1 cup onion, finely chopped
1/3 cup milk

1 egg, beaten
1 1/2 tsp salt
1/4 tsp pepper
3/4 tsp allspice
1/4 tsp nutmeg

(sauce)
2 tbsp flour
1/2 cup beef stock
1 cup heavy cream

Directions:

Mix all the meat ball ingredients and form into 36 balls. Brown in batches in frying pan with olive oil. When brown, remove to a bowl.

When the meatballs are all browned, add the flour to the drippings in the frying pan and combine well. Remove the pan from the heat for two minutes to cool slightly then stir in the beef stock and mix well. Slowly stir in the cream and cook until slightly thickened.

Return the meat balls to the sauce.

Serve over noodles.

9

Fish and Seafood

Salmon Cakes

(Notebook 1, pp 33)

Ingredients:

(poaching liquid)

4 cups water

1 cup dry white wine

4 sprigs celery leaves

6 sprigs parsley

6 whole pepper corns

1 tsp salt

(salmon cakes)

1 pound salmon fillet

1/4 cups bread crumbs

1 tsp thyme

1 tsp oregano

1/2 tsp dry mustard

Pinch of cayenne pepper

Salt and pepper to taste

1 cup mayonnaise

1/2 cup finely diced onion

1/2 cup finely diced celery

1 tablespoon coarsely chopped capers

1 tablespoon finely chopped parsley

1 tsp Worcestershire sauce

1 large egg, beaten

(coating)

1 cup bread crumbs

(for frying)

2 tbsp cooking oil

Directions:

(to poach fish)

Combine the water, wine, celery leaves, parsley, peppercorns and salt in a fish poacher or large pan and bring to a boil. Reduce to a simmer and poach the salmon fillet for 10 minutes until it flakes. Remove from poaching liquid, flake into a bowl and allow to cool.

(to make the salmon cakes)

Combine the flaked salmon with the remaining ingredients and form into 10 patties two and one-half inches in diameter and three-quarters of an inch thick.

Roll in the crumbs, place on platter and refrigerate for one hour. The fish and seasonings will be nearly liquid and it is necessary to refrigerate the patties so they hold together.

Fry in the oil about three minutes on a side over medium heat. Be careful not to over-brown them.

Salmon croquette, mashed potatoes and Green Giant Mexicorn (corn with red and green pepper)

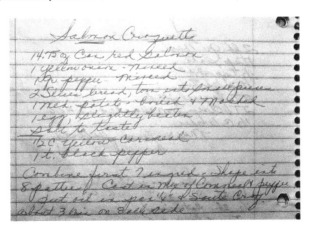

Salmon Croquettes

(Notebook 1, pp 20, Cards #1)

These salmon cakes (Joan called them croquettes) call for mashed potatoes, which gives them a really interesting texture. They fry very nicely too. Joan must have liked salmon cakes. We found five recipes for them in Notebook 1 (pages 20, 25, 26, 33 and 45). They included one (pp 26) from Linda,[34] who got it while she was attending Empire Beauty School in Mechanicsburg in 1995. She got it from a friend who was from an African-American family in Carlisle. It's unique in that it is seasoned with one eighth teaspoon each of red, white and black pepper. Joan made a note in her recipe that she added mayonnaise, instant mashed potatoes and an additional egg.

We also found a recipe for salmon cakes in Florence's recipe box (#1), but it was quite different. It called for a cup of rice instead of the bread and potatoes in Joan's recipe. Florence's recipe card has "Joan" on it.

We've pictured a salmon cake on a plate with Green Giant Mexicorn, something that both Linda and Ken Jr. remember. Green Giant still makes it.

Today, modern cooks probably find it hard to envision life in Joan's early years when vegetables were considered a necessary, but neglected secondary part of a meal. Canned vegetables had been, for most of the early 20th century, the fast solution to the "you-must-eat-your-vegetables" problem. Grandmothers, born in the 19th century boiled vegetables until they turned to mush. Canned vegetables were an alternative when anything fresh was out of season or considered too expensive in the grocery store.

Frozen vegetables, which came into wide use in the early 1950s, were considered a huge improvement and it became possible to rent frozen food lockers and stock them with frozen meat and vegetables, often part of a plan offered by businesses that provided the locker facilities. The plans typically offered discounts for buying bulk quantities. Buying half carcasses of beef, cut to your specifications, became popular as well. Home "chest" freezers were still a way off and the freezer in the refrigerator could only hold so much.

Joan served mostly frozen vegetables when fresh ones were not in season. She did cook canned vegetables as well. Typically, she found more interesting mixes. Linda and Ken Jr. remembered that in addition to the Mexicorn, Joan also bought Leseur brand small peas and Delmonte Seasoned French Cut Green Beans with onion, red pepper and garlic. All three are still available.

Ingredients:
(croquettes)
1 medium size potato

14.75 oz can red salmon
1 cup yellow onion, finely diced
1 cup green pepper, finely diced
2 slices bread, cut in one-inch squares
1 egg, beaten
salt

(coating)
1/2 cup yellow cornmeal
1 tsp black pepper

Directions;

Peel and thinly slice the potato. Boil it in water until it's soft (five to 10 minutes). Mash it and cool.

Mix thoroughly the salmon, onion, green pepper, bread, mashed potatoes and egg. Form into eight patties. Combine the corn meal and pepper and coat the croquettes with it thickly.

Fry, one at a time, about three minutes on each side in one-half inch of oil in frying pan.

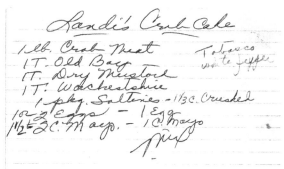

Landis Crab Cakes

(Cards #2)

Joan obviously got this recipe from Bobby Landis, the cook who was her partner in their Emmaus restaurant, BJ's Steak and Crab (1991-93).

We ate these in the restaurant. They came to the table drenched in butter.

It's a unique recipe since it calls for a huge amount of mayonnaise — one and one-half to two cups. Joan noted on the recipe card that she used one cup. There seem to be two styles of crab cakes out there: those that call for a lot of mayo and those that call for one to one and one-half tablespoons. Bobby's crab cakes were more like a batter when they were mixed up and ready to put in the pan.

Ingredients:

1 pound crab meat (I prefer lump and steer away from the cheaper claw)

1 tbsp Old Bay seasoning

1 tbsp dry mustard

1 tbsp Worcestershire sauce

1 1/3 cups crushed saltines

1 egg

1 cup mayonnaise

Tabasco sauce to taste (I used 1/2 tsp)

white pepper

salt to taste

Directions:

Mix all ingredients. Form into eight crab cakes. Fry in one-fourth inch of hot oil in a frying pan.

10

Vegetables

Joan used fresh vegetables when they were inexpensive and available. She used frozen and canned ones often. Vegetables were a bit of an "issue" with Linda. She liked some, although she had a narrow range: Le Sueur canned peas, canned French cut green beans, canned Del Monte seasoned green beans, canned Green Giant Mexacali corn (with red pepper), frozen mixed vegetables (especially in Hamburger Vegetable Soup), John Cope's Dried Corn (stewed, not in the pudding form) and Campbell's condensed tomato soup.

Joan wasn't especially loyal to any brand and generally bought what was on sale, what she had a coupon for or, in some cases, marked-down dented cans.

Pepper Cabbage

(Boyertown Cookery, pp 32)

Joan had no recipe for this but there was one in her *Boyertown Cookery* charity cookbook. Linda's youngest brother Chad said she made it with red pepper instead of green. I grew up eating it with green pepper and cabbage.

Ingredients:
4 cups cabbage, grated
1 green pepper, grated (red pepper optional)
1/4 cup grated celery
1/4 cup apple cider vinegar
1/4 cup sugar
1/4 tsp salt
1/4 tsp pepper

Directions:
Grate the cabbage and pepper. Mix the sugar, vinegar salt and pepper until sugar is dissolved. Stir into the vegetables.

It is best if it stands for at least 24 hours before serving.

Green Bean Casserole

There's no recipe for this in Joan's collection. In her day everybody seemed to know how to make it from memory. This might be the most popular vegetable recipe in the American home cooking repertoire. It was created in 1955 by Dorcas B. Reilly, in the Campbell Soup Company test kitchen. When Reilly died in October of 2018, her passing was a major news story.

The casserole is usually made in the save-time-just-add-a-can-of-soup style of cooking that became wildly popular in the 1950s and is still with us. Recipes using convenience ingredients like canned soup, often came from food company test kitchen recipes. They appeared on product packaging and in premium cookbooks, newspaper and magazine food sections. The entire trend was reflected, and probably further popularized, by the publication of the 1951 *Can Opener Cookbook*, by Poppy Cannon.[35]

Linda's ex-husband Al Gartner, has been bringing this casserole to family holiday dinners in Carlisle for many years. It always gets eaten.

Preheat oven to: 375 degrees
Baking dish: 9 by 13-inch, (three quart)

Ingredients:
(sauce)
3 tbsp butter

1 clove garlic
3 tbsp flour
2 cups milk
1/2 tsp salt
1/2 tsp thyme
Bread crumbs
3 oz French fried onion rings
1/2 cup parmesan cheese

(vegetables)
1/2 pound mushrooms (Cremini are good) cut in 1/2-inch pieces
2 cups coarsely chopped onion
1 pound fresh green beans, cleaned and cut into one-inch pieces

Directions:

Melt butter in a large sauce pan. Add the garlic, allowing it to sizzle for a few seconds then stir in the flour. Stir to incorporate. Add the milk and stir until the sauce thickens.

Add the salt, thyme and mushrooms to the sauce and simmer while you cook the beans.

Bring two cups of water to a boil in a sauce pan. Add the beans and cook them eight minutes, or until they are just cooked. Do not overcook.

Drain the beans and add them to the other vegetables in the sauce.

Grease a nine-by-13-inch baking dish and sprinkle the greased surfaces with bread crumbs. Pour in the sauce and vegetables. Bake at 375 degrees for 25 minutes.

Sprinkle the Parmesan cheese and fried onions on top and return to the oven for another five minutes.

(handwritten recipe card)

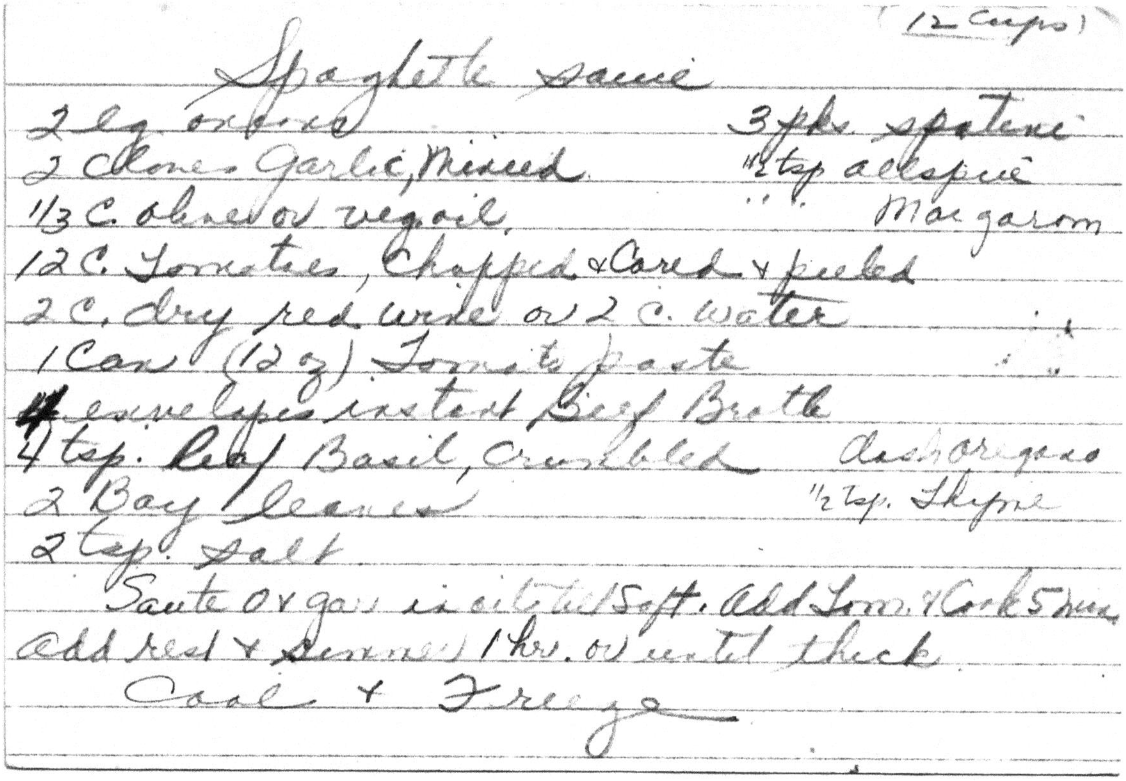

> (12 cups)
>
> Spaghetti sauce
> 2 lg onions   3 pks spatini
> 2 cloves garlic, minced   ½ tsp allspice
> 1/3 C. olive or veg oil,   " " Marjoram
> 12 C. Tomatoes, chopped & cored & peeled
> 2 C. dry red wine or 2 c. water
> 1 can (12 oz) Tomato paste
> 4 envelopes instant Beef Broth
> 4 tsp. leaf Basil, crumbled   dash oregano
> 2 Bay leaves   ½ tsp. Thyme
> 2 tsp. salt
>   Saute or gas in oil hot 15 ft. Add Tom. & cook 5 min.
> add rest & simmer 1 hr. or until thick.
>   Cool + Freeze

Spaghetti Sauce

(Cards #2)

Joan's tomato sauce was unique because she used Spatini seasoning mix and added a little cocoa. As we mentioned earlier, Spatini is no longer available, but there are copycat recipes

available on the World Wide Web. The main ingredients seem to be corn starch, powdered sugar and beef bouillon in addition to the expected Italian seasonings: garlic, onion, pepper, oregano and thyme.

The cocoa is not mentioned in any recipe, but Linda was well familiar with her mother's practice of putting it in her tomato sauce.

Joan's recipe card gives directions for making 12 cups of sauce from fresh tomatoes. We cut it down to make about a quart of sauce using two 16-oz cans of chopped tomatoes.

Ingredients:
1 cup onions, chopped
1 cloves garlic, mashed
3 tbsp olive oil
1/2 cup dry red wine
4 cups canned, chopped tomatoes
4 oz tomato paste
1 tsp beef soup base
1 tsp basil
1 bay leaves
1/2 tsp salt
1/4 tsp allspice
1/4 tsp marjoram
1/4 tsp thyme
1/8 tsp oregano
1/2 tsp cocoa

(ingredients equivalent to Spatini seasoning mix)
1 tsp beef soup base
1 1/2 tsp powdered sugar
1 tsp corn starch
1/4 tsp oregano
1/4 tsp thyme
1/4 tsp onion powder
1/8 tsp garlic powder
pepper

Directions:
Sauté the onion and garlic in the olive oil until they are soft. Turn heat to high and pour in the wine. Reduce by one half.

Add the tomatoes and remaining ingredients and simmer one hour or until thick.

Béchamel sauce substitute for condensed soup

Joan used condensed soups – mushroom, chicken and celery – in many of her recipes. They are really just a convenience-food substitute for Béchamel sauce. Making real Béchamel sauce with mushrooms, chicken or celery only takes minutes and the flavor is vastly better.

Ingredients:
3 tbsp butter
1/2 cup finely diced celery, chicken or mushrooms
1/2 cup finely chopped onion
1 1/2 tbsp corn starch
1 1/2 tbsp flour
1 1/2 cups milk or half and half
1 small bay leaf
1/2 tsp celery seed, ground to a powder with a mortar and pestle (for cream of celery soup only)

Directions:
Melt the butter in a sauce pan and sauté the onion over medium heat until it's translucent (five minutes). Reduce heat and stir in the corn starch and flour, mixing well, then add the milk or half-and-half. Bring to a boil to thicken.
Stir in bay leaf and:
-- For a substitute for cream of celery soup add celery seed and celery when sautéing the onion.
-- For a substitute for mushroom soup add chopped mushrooms with the onion.
-- For a substitute for chicken soup, add chopped cooked chicken with the onion.
Allow to simmer for 10 minutes. Remove the bay leaf before using.

12

Desserts

Booze Balls

(Notebook 10, pp 1)

I can remember these from Joan's holiday celebrations after I joined the family in 1991. Linda doesn't remember them, but that would make sense since she wouldn't exactly have a childhood memory for a dessert that contained alcohol.

Note: This recipe calls for milk chocolate chips to be melted. If you have never melted milk chocolate before, be aware that milk chocolate, when overheated, seizes up — turns into a granular solid mass that must be completely cooled and reheated (carefully) to melt. So, heat the chocolate in the microwave using three or four 10-second intervals, stirring between each.

Ingredients:

6 oz semi-sweet chocolate chips or bits

3 tbsp Karo (light or dark)

1/2 cup sugar

1/2 cup liquor (some possibilities include rum and whiskey, as well as liqueurs such as créme de menthe)

3-4 oz chopped nuts (walnuts or pecans are good) A food processor is good for chopping them.

11 oz (one box) Vanilla Wafers, chopped finely. Again, a food processor is good for this.

Powdered sugar for dusting.

Directions:

Carefully melt chocolate chips, in microwave. Heat for 10 second interval, stir, heat again until melted

Add Karo, sugar and liquor. Stir to blend all together.

Blend in nuts then the Vanilla Wafer crumbs.

Wet your hands under the tap then roll into balls about one and one-half inches in diameter, roll in the powdered sugar and refrigerate before serving. It would be best to store these in a sealed container to keep the alcohol from evaporating.

Chocolate Peanut Butter Fudge

(Cards #2)

This is a very simple fudge recipe, unusually simple. The ingredients are heated only a minimum of time then it's refrigerated. Linda remembers it as "refrigerator fudge." She said "my mother would never have taken the time to stir fudge on the stove."

The "Stella" listed on the recipe is Joan's aunt Estella (Rothenberger) Gift.

Baking dish: 8 by 8 inch

Ingredients:
1/2 pound butter (2 sticks)
4 cups powdered sugar
1/2 pound peanut butter (3/4 cup)
1 cup cocoa
1 tbsp vanilla

Directions:
Melt butter and combine with the cocoa over medium heat. Add peanut butter and vanilla and heat to boiling. Add the sugar, one cup at a time, returning to a boil after each addition. Stir constantly to prevent the fudge from burning.

Pour into greased eight-by-eight-inch pan and refrigerate.

Pumpkin Cream Cheese Jelly Roll

(Notebook 9, pp 40)

Linda has been making these at Christmas for some time. When she first tried the recipe, the cake part didn't appear to be big enough, so she doubled the recipe. It made a HUGE roll and was a Christmastime joke for years: "remember when mom made that enormous pumpkin roll."

The recipe calls for the cake to be baked in then dumped out onto a dish towel dusted heavily with powdered sugar. Joan gave Linda special dish towel that is reserved just for this pumpkin roll.

Preheat oven to: 375 degrees

Ingredients:
(roll)
1 cup flour
1/2 teaspoon cinnamon
3/4 cup sugar
1 1/2 tsp baking powder
1/2 tsp ground nutmeg
3/4 cup canned pumpkin
1/4 tsp salt
4 eggs at room temperature
10x sugar
(Filling)
12 oz cream cheese at room temperature
1 tsp vanilla
2/3 cup sugar
1/4 cup mini chocolate chips
1/4 cup slivered almonds, toasted and chopped coarsely

Directions:
Line jelly roll pan with wax paper or parchment and spray with cooking spray.
Beat eggs in a large bowl for two minutes or until thickened.
Add sugar, one tablespoon at a time, and beat on low speed for five to seven minutes until very thick and lemon colored. Add pumpkin and beat on low speed until it's just combined.
Fold in dry ingredients then spread in jelly roll pan.
Bake 375 for 10-12 minutes.
Spread a towel with 10X sugar and dump the cake carefully on it. Sprinkle with more 10X sugar. Roll up in towel and let cool for one hour.
For filling: Beat the cream cheese, sugar and vanilla until creamy — five to eight minutes. Stir in chocolate chips and almonds
Unroll the cake on the towel and spread evenly with the filling. Re-roll and refrigerate for four hours or overnight.

Fastnachts dusted with sugar

Fastnachts

(Notebook 11, pp 64, 11, Notebook 9, pp 73, Cards #2 and twice in Cards #1)

Fastnachts are deep-fried pastries traditionally served in many areas of Pennsylvania with Pennsylvania Dutch traditions on Shrove Tuesday, the day before the beginning of Lent.

They are sold by churches as fundraisers as well as by grocery stores and bakeries in the south east and south-central parts of the state on "Fastnacht Day."

A search of the World Wide Web turned up major feature stories about Fastnacht Day in 2019 in newspapers and their Web sites in the southeastern third of Pennsylvania in:

- — Pocono Record of Stroudsburg
- — Times Herald of Norristown
- — Eagle of Reading
- — Lancaster Journal, Lancaster
- — Daily News, Lebanon
- — Daily Record of York
- — Patriot-News of Harrisburg
- — Daily Item of Sunbury
- — Sun Gazette, Williamsport

— Public Opinion, Chambersburg

— Times, Gettysburg

— Herald Mail, Hagerstown, Md. (also circulates in south central Pa.)

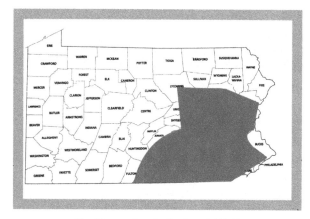

Newspapers in Philadelphia, Pittsburgh and State College mentioned organizations or bakeries selling fastnachts in brief columns.

Using the extent of the Fastnacht Day front page news coverage, one could draw a map of the "Pennsylvania Fastnacht Belt."

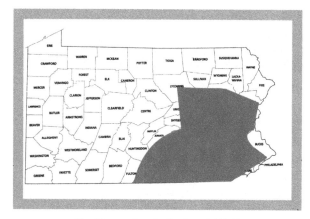

The Pennsylvania Fastnacht Belt

Linda remembers that Joan made them in the years she wasn't employed outside the house. Joan had five recipes for them. The recipe in notebook 9 has "Anna" after the title as does a card with the identical recipe in Joan's file card box #2. We have no idea who Anna was.

Linda said:

““ *I remember she would be making them when I came home from work and the house would* ”” *smell really good. She made them the day before (Fastnacht Day) and on the day. We'd pig out on them. She'd give them to people too.*

The dough is very interesting, and not especially easy to work with. It contains mashed potatoes which, when beaten, give the fastnachts a pleasant, chewy consistency. The dough also is very wet, which makes a bit difficult to manipulate after it has been cut to shape and left to rise a second time.

After the first rising, the directions call for the dough to be dusted well with flour, rolled out, cut into rectangles, and allowed to rise a second time. It would be a good idea to separate the individual pieces of dough by at least an inch so the finished, raised fastnachts don't stick to one another before they can be scooped up and put in the hot fat.

Since fastnachts often are fried in the morning, it is important that you are aware that the dough must be mixed up the night before.

(Above recipe cut in half)
Ingredients:
2 medium size potatoes, peeled and sliced
1 1/2 cups water
3/4 cups granulated sugar
1 egg
1/4 cup butter
1/2 cup milk
1 tbsp yeast
1/4 tsp salt
5 cups flour

Directions:
(The night before)
Cook the potatoes in the water until they are quite soft — 25 minutes. Set the pan aside to cool completely.

In the bowl of a mixer, beat the sugar, eggs and butter.

Drain the cooled potatoes (saving the water) and mash them. Add the milk, yeast, salt, potatoes and potato water (add water to make one and one-half cups if necessary) to the mixer bowl and mix well.

Add the flour one cup at a time with the mixer at slow speed, then beat one minute at high speed to activate the starch and give the proper texture.

The dough will be very moist.

Cover the mixer bowl with plastic film and set in a warm room to rise over night.

(The day the fastnachts are to be fried)

Scoop the risen dough out onto a counter that has been covered with flour. Roll out into a rectangle 12 by 32 inches, making the dough about one-half inch thick.

Cut the dough into rectangles about three by four inches (cut it into 32 pieces). I did this by cutting the large rectangle into eighths in the long direction then fourths in the short direction.

Using a spatula or side of a chef knife, separate the dough rectangles from each other by at least an inch. When they rise a second time, they will adhere to each other if they are not separated.

Cover the rectangles with plastic film wrap to keep them from drying out.

After the dough has risen a second time (one hour) heat the oil in a deep-fat fryer to 375 degrees.

Carefully scoop up the fastnachts with a spatula that has been oiled and place them carefully in the hot fat. They will be very soft.

Fry them three or four at a time until they are a medium brown (two minutes on a side).

After they have fried, dip them out of the fat, allowing them to drain, and put them on a rack over a plate to drain further and cool.

The fastnachts may be eaten as they are or coated with:

— powdered sugar

— granulated sugar

— icing

— jam

— molasses

Lemon Lush

(Cards #2)

This was apparently a favorite dessert in Joan's household. Linda and Ken Jr. emphatically asked for it to be included and Rick remembered it well. It's from the Poppy Cannon school of cooking: using convenience ingredients — Cool Whip and instant pudding.

Cool Whip imitation whipped cream (called a "whipped topping") was first put on the market in 1966 and the Lemon Lush recipe is on the Kraft Web site today.[36]

We found the same Lemon Lush recipe in a 1973 charity cookbook published by the Alumnae Association of Penn Hall Junior College in Chambersburg, Pa.[37]

We know the exactly where Joan got the recipe: page A9 of the *Pottstown Mercury* of June 29, 1982. We found the clipped recipe in her recipe box (#2). It also was copied onto a card in the box. She apparently gave it to her mother Florence since there was an identical copy of the recipe in her recipe file box with the notation "Joan."

Joan apparently lengthened the baking time for the crust, switched from pecans to walnuts and made it in a nine-by-13-inch baking dish instead of an 11-by-17. The original probably would have come out more like a bar cookie where Joan's was more like a pie.

It's an excellent recipe, especially the crust which is butter, flour and finely chopped walnuts.

Preheat oven to: 400 degrees
Baking Pan: 9 by 13-inch pan

Ingredients:
(crust)
2 sticks butter
2 cups flour
1 cup walnuts, chopped finely

(filling)
8 oz cream cheese
1 cup 10X sugar
1 cup from a 16 oz container of Cool Whip
2 instant lemon pudding mixes (small boxes)
3 cups milk

Directions:
(crust)
Combine thoroughly the butter, flour and walnuts. Press into the bottom of a greased nine-by-13-inch pan.

Bake at 400 degrees for 20 minutes. Remove from oven and allow it to cool.

(filing)
Beat cream cheese and sugar until they are smooth. Fold in one cup of the Cool Whip and spread on the baked crust.

Mix the pudding and milk and beat until it's smooth. Spread on top.

Spread the remaining Cool Whip on top and refrigerate OR, refrigerate and top individual servings with Cool Whip.

Linda's Dessert

(Cards #3)

Preheat oven to: 375 degrees
Bake in: 9-by-13-inch pan

Ingredients:
(bottom and top layer)
2 cups waffle pretzels, crushed

3/4 cup sugar

3/4 cup (1 1/2 sticks) butter, melted

(cream cheese filling)

2 packages Dream Whip (Note: there are two packages in each box of Dream Whip)

1 tsp vanilla

8 oz cream cheese

1 cup 10x sugar

1 can cherry pie filling

Directions:

(bottom and top layers)

Mix the pretzels, sugar and butter. Reserve one half cup for the top crust and pack the other half in a nine-by-13-inch baking dish. Bake at 375 degrees for 10 minutes. Cool completely.

(cream cheese filling)

Mix the Dream Whip and vanilla. Add the cream cheese and 10x sugar and beat until it's creamy.

(assembly)

Spread half the cream cheese filling on the pretzel layer in the baking pan. Cover with the cherry pie filling.

Cover that with the other half of the cream cheese filling.

Cover that with the reserved one-half cup of pretzel mixture.

Refrigerate overnight.

13

Cakes

Joan and cakes

Linda recalled:

*" My mother didn't buy a lot of instant stuff. She hated that prepared stuff. She never made "
a box cake or used canned icing. If she went to a bake sale and bought a cake that turned out
to be a box cake, she was mad.*

*She always bought Jean Aflerbach's cakes. Everybody did because Jean always made them
from scratch.*

Jean was a neighbor in the row house in Trumbauersville.

Monkey Cake

(Notebook 13, pp 30)

This is an easy-to-make recipe that uses refrigerated biscuits. Everyone loves it.

Linda remembered that Joan started making monkey cake in her "Tupperware lady" days – she sold Tupperware in the years before 1977. We found the recipe in notebook 13 (possibly the oldest), which Joan originally used for Tupperware party ideas. After 16 pages of Tupperware notes, it changed to a recipe notebook.

The Monkey Cake recipe even calls for the use of a Tupperware bowl to coat the pieces of biscuit with cinnamon and sugar: "Shake, coating each piece with cinnamon and sugar in Lg. T-Ware mixing bowl."

A recipe for "monkey bread" – a similar recipe but without the sugar and cinnamon coating – first shows up in a search of American newspapers in a 1956 story in the Fort Worth, Tex. *Star-Telegram*: "Ft. Worth Junior Leaguers Offer Sparkling Cook Book."[38]

In 1960, a column in the *Atlanta Constitution* credits the actress and comedian Zasu Pitts (1894-1963) with the recipe, which is included in the piece.[39]

In a 1966 column in the *Detroit Free Press,* cookbook writer Poppy Cannon (author of *The Can Opener Cookbook*, 1951) said the recipe originated in Louisiana or Tennessee. Cannon gave the first recipe for a sweet version similar to Joan's.[40]

Preheat oven to: 350 degrees
Baking pan: tube pan

Ingredients:
4 cans refrigerator biscuits
2 tsp cinnamon
2/3 cups sugar

(butter-sugar coating)
1 cups sugar
1 1/2 sticks butter

(optional)
Raisins and nuts

Directions:
Mix the cinnamon and sugar in a large bowl.
Melt the butter for the butter-sugar coating, add the sugar and bring to a boil.
Open the biscuits and cut each one into fourths. Place in the bowl with the cinnamon and sugar and coat them well.
Place half the coated biscuit pieces in a tube pan mixing well with half the nuts or raisins if using. Sprinkle with half the butter-sugar coating. Add the other half of the coated biscuits and remaining nuts or raisins, mixing well, then sprinkle with the other half of the butter-sugar coating.
Bake in a 350-degree oven for 45 minutes.
Place a platter over the tube pan and invert to dump the cake out.

Shoo Fly Cake

(Cards #2 and Notebook 11, pp 23)

This cake is, obviously, shoo fly pie made without a pie crust. Possibly it is the ancestor of shoo fly pie. It would be no big leap of the imagination to bake it in a pie crust.

There was a "Centennial cake" created at the 1875 Centennial Celebration in Philadelphia, which Pennsylvania food Historian William Woys Weaver believes was the inspiration for shoo-fly pie.[41] The pie was first documented about 1880.

Preheat oven to: 350 degrees

Baking dish: 9-by-13-inch (3 quart) baking dish

Ingredients:

4 cups of flour

3 cups of brown sugar

1 cup butter

1 cup molasses

2 tsp baking soda
2 cups boiling water

Directions:

Combine the flour, brown sugar and butter, mixing until it is the consistency of coarse crumbs. Measure out one and one half cups of the crumbs and set them aside.

To the remaining crumbs, add the molasses, baking soda and boiling water. Combine well and pour into a nine-by-13 (3 quart) baking dish.

Top with the reserved one and one-half cups of crumbs and bake at 350 degrees for 35 minutes.

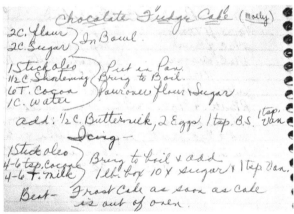

Chocolate Fudge Cake

(Notebook 11, pp 11)

This recipe is marked "(Molly)" meaning that Joan got it from her aunt Molly – Marion (Rothenberger) Taylor. Aunt Molly was a nurse who lived in Boyertown then, later in life, in Landisburg.

Preheat oven to: 350 degrees
Baking dish: 9-by-13-inch (3 quart) baking dish

Ingredients:
(cake)
2 cups flour
2 cups sugar
1 cup (2 sticks) butter
6 tbsp cocoa
1 cup water
1/2 cup buttermilk
2 beaten eggs
1 tsp baking soda
1 tsp vanilla

(Icing)
1/2 cup (1 stick) butter
4 tsp cocoa
4 tablespoons milk
1 pound 10x sugar
1 tsp vanilla

Directions:
(For cake:)
Combine the flour and sugar in a bowl and set aside.

In sauce pan, melt butter, mix in the cocoa, then add the water and combine well. Combine with the flour and sugar that were set aside.

Mix in the buttermilk, beaten egg, baking soda and vanilla. Pour into a nine-by-13-inch (3 quart) pan

Bake at 350 degrees for 30-35 minutes then put on icing while the cake is still hot.

(For icing:)
Melt the butter in a sauce pan then add the cocoa and milk. bring to a boil, remove from heat and stir in the 10x sugar and vanilla. Return to medium heat and still until well-combined and liquid.

Pour the icing over the hot cake and spread evenly.

Moravian Cake

(Cards #2 and #4, *Corps* Cookbook pp 146 and Notebook 11, pp 17)

Linda remembers that many friends and family members made this because it was simple and only required readily available ingredients. This recipe also evolved. Linda's recipe box (#4) contained a version she got from Joan at some time in the 1980s, with minor changes to amounts of ingredients and a baking time of 30-35 minutes.

Preheat oven to: 350 degrees

Baking pan: 9-by-13-inch (3 quart) baking dish

Ingredients:

(For cake)

2 cups sugar

4 cups flour

4 tsp baking powder

2 cups milk

2 tbsp oil

(For topping)

4 tbsp butter

1 cup brown sugar

1 tbsp cinnamon

Directions:

Combine sugar, flour and baking powder in mixing bowl. Add milk and oil. Beat until it forms a thick batter, about one minute.

Pour in nine-by-13-inch baking dish and dot with butter. Sprinkle brown sugar then the cinnamon evenly over the top.

Bake 350 for 30-35 minutes.

Joan's great granddaughter JayLin Gartner putting Apies
cakes in the oven to bake

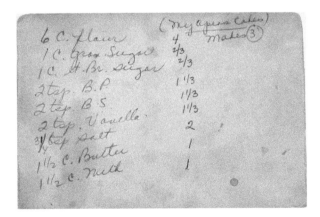

Apies Cake

(Cards #2, *Corps* cookbook, pp 130)

This is a very unique recipe. There were 23 variations in Joan's library: 16 in three of the charity cookbooks and seven more in notebooks and file card boxes. It seems to be local to the Boyertown area, and is probably more than 300 years old.

The breakfast coffee cake was called Apieskuchen in Switzerland where "Apies" is a Swiss dialect word for the church holiday of Epiphany. William Woys Weaver, who described it in his book *Pennsylvania Dutch Country Cooking*,[42] believes that it was brought to Bally in Berks County (about six miles north of Florence's home in Boyertown) by Swiss Catholics in the early 1700s.

In the *Boyertown Cookery* charity cookbook, published in 1978 by the Boyertown Historical Society (with five recipes for it), a one-page description of "Apeas cake" quotes a Mr. Watson, writing in the *Annals of Philadelphia* in 1832, as saying a woman named Ann Page baked the cakes and stamped her initials, "A,P." on them at that time.[43]

There is no Apies cake recipe in the 1975 *Heirloom Cookbook* published by the Quakertown Historical Society. Quakertown, where Joan moved when she was in high school. Quakertown is 16 miles east of Bally. There are, however, nine recipes in the *Schwenkfelder Cook Book* published by a church in the community of Palm just four miles northeast of Bally.

Joan's aunt Estella Gift submitted it for the *Corps* cookbook in 1983. Lansdale is 23 miles southeast of Bally.

Joan apparently created her own recipe using half white and half brown sugar. It's titled "My Apeas Cakes Makes (3)" and appears on the back of a card in her recipe box (#2). On the front of the card is a recipe titled "White A.P.'s Cakes" and is attributed to "Elsie."

Joan gave her mother and her daughter "her" recipe. It is unlikely that it was the first time Florence saw an Apies cake recipe. Florence and her sisters Estella and Molly regularly went to Joan's house to make them in the late 60s. Florence had Joan's recipe in her recipe box titled "Joan's A.B. (sic) Cake."

Linda copied two recipes for it (Joan's and her great aunt Estella's) into the first kitchen note book that we began to keep when we moved in together in 1992. She prefers Estella's (given here) which calls for all brown sugar.

The variety of names on the recipes in Joan's collection is laughable when one knows the origin. In the *Corps* Cookbook, Joan's Aunt Estella named it "A-P Cake," and we've seen it called "Apeas Cake," "A.P. cake," "Dutch Apeas Cake," "A.P.'s Cake" and "Ann Page" cake, the last possibly from the 1832 Philadelphia connection.

It's a unique recipe for another reason: it calls for baking soda to be mixed with vinegar before blending it in to the batter. One would think that the vinegar would neutralize the rising action of the baking soda since it causes it to foam. But it doesn't. The cakes rise properly and there is a very subtle flavor from the vinegar in them.

The use of baking soda as a leavening agent only dates back to the late 19th century. Before that, pearlash (lye basically) was used.

Peter Rose, a historian of Dutch colonial cooking in the New World believes that the use of pearlash was a professional secret of European bakers. He suggests that the secret slipped out from Dutch bakers near Albany, N.Y., in the mid 1700s and home bakers began using it.[44]

The first reference to it in an American cookbook was in Amelia Simmons' 1796 cookbook *American Cookery*.[45] Simmons calls for "pearlash" in three gingerbread recipes. In one she calls for it to be dissolved in water and one dissolved in milk.

I'm conjecturing that cooks originally dissolved the pearlash in vinegar to make it begin producing the carbon dioxide that makes dough rise. Recipes at the time called for the pearlash to be dissolved in milk, sour milk or buttermilk. When baking soda replaced pearlash, the chemical reaction was no longer necessary, but those baking Apies cakes, being accustomed to the vinegar, continued its use because it was in their recipes.

Preheat oven to: 350 degrees

Baking pans: 9-inch pie pans

Ingredients:

1 cup brown sugar

1/2 cup (1 stick) softened butter

2 cups flour

1/4 tsp salt

1 tsp baking soda

1 tsp vinegar

1/2 cup plus 2 tbsp milk

Directions:

Cream the brown sugar and butter in a mixer.

Add flour, and salt.

Mix the soda and vinegar in a cup and add it to the milk.

Add the liquid ingredients to the mixer bowl and mix.

Press into two nine-inch pie pans and bake at 350 degrees for 35 minutes or bake in three six-inch pie pans for 20 minutes.

Chocolate Chip Cake

(Cards #1, #2, #4 and Notebook 11, pp 18)

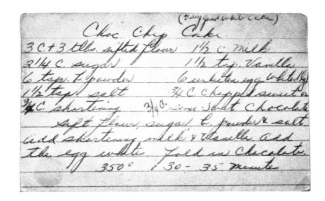

Linda remembers that Joan commonly served this as a birthday cake. The recipe may have been in the family for some time. We found a copy in what we take to be Florence's handwriting in the oldest recipe box (#1).

Preheat oven to: 350 degrees

Baking pans: two 8-inch layer pans

Ingredients:

3 cups and 3 tablespoons of flour

2 1/4 cups sugar

6 tsp baking powder

1 1/2 tsp salt

3/4 cups shortening

1 1/2 cups milk

1 1/2 tsp vanilla

6 egg whites

3/4 cup mini chocolate chips

Directions:

Mix flour, sugar, baking powder and salt in the bowl of a mixer.

Add the shortening, milk and vanilla and beat. Add egg whites and beat again.

Fold in chocolate chips.

Divide the batter into two layer pans that have been greased, floured and lined with wax paper covering the bottoms.

Bake at 350 degrees for 40 minutes, then cool.

Place one layer on a platter and cover the top with frosting of choice. Place the second layer on top and cover with frosting on top and sides.

Apple Sauce Cake

(Cards #1 and #2)

Joan made this for many years. I remember eating it, so that means she was still baking it after 1992. It was one of Linda's favorites and she recalled making it after starting her own family (1982). Joan might have gotten the recipe from her mother since we found the identical recipe in Florence's handwriting — including the orange butter icing and note, "Alga," to the right of the title.

As one would guess from the name, it has apple sauce in it which makes it quite moist. It's a device that works the same in carrot cake, zucchini bread and banana bread — adding puréed or grated fruit or vegetables to a batter.

This appears to have been a known recipe nationwide and in central and eastern Pennsylvania for some time. The recipe Joan had, and the one in the *Corps* cookbook seem to be unique in that they include nutmeg.

There are similar recipes for an applesauce cake in:

— the 1933 first edition of *Joy of Cooking* (pp 238) as well as the 1964 fifth edition (pp 629).

— The 1950 *Pennsylvania Grange Cookbook*, but with the addition of molasses (pp 45). It was submitted by Mrs. George W. Howard of the Vincent Grange 1664. The grange possibly was in East Vincent Township in northern Chester County not far from Boyertown.

— The 1974 *Great Radio Ask Your Neighbor Cook Book* (pp 33) published by WLSH in Lansford. It was submitted by Anne Shemansky of Frackville, which is in Schuylkill County.

— The 1983 *Corps* cookbook (pp 135), from Boyertown.

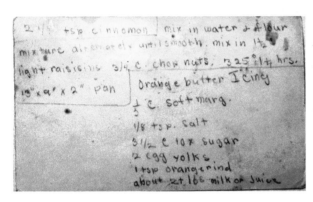

The recipe appears in the 1918 *Metropolitan Life Cook Book*, (Published by the Metropolitan Life Insurance Company) on page 57. We found a crumbling copy of this in Joan's effects. It must have belonged to her grandmother Suzanna.

We also found an applesauce cake recipe in the 1976 facsimile reprint of the 1911 *Franklin County Charity Benefit Cook Book* (pp 91). That book originally was published in Chambersburg as a fund raiser for "The Hospital, The Children's Aid Society and the Old Folks' Home." It was submitted by Mrs. J. E. Denlinger.

Preheat oven to: 325 degrees
Baking dish: 9-by-13-inch (3 quart) baking dish

Ingredients:
3/4 cups shortening or butter
2 1/4 cups sugar
3 eggs
2 1/4 cups sweetened apple sauce
water (1/2 cup plus one tbsp if using butter and 3/4 cup if using shortening)
4 cups flour
3 tsp baking powder
3/4 tsp baking soda
2 1/4 tsp salt
3/4 tsp cloves
3/4 tsp cinnamon
3/4 tsp nutmeg
1 1/2 cups golden raisins
3/4 cups walnuts or pecans

(for icing)
1/3 cup butter, at room temperature
1/8 tsp salt
3 1/2 cups 10X sugar
3 egg yolks
1 tsp orange zest
2 tbsp milk or orange juice

Directions:

In a mixer bowl, cream the shortening or butter and sugar. Add the eggs and mix until light and fluffy. Add the apple sauce and mix until well combined.

Add the remaining ingredients (except the nuts and raisins) and beat until well combined.

Stir the nuts and raisins into the batter by hand.

Pour into baking dish that has been greased and floured.

Bake 325 degrees for one hour and 15 minutes.

Allow to cool.

(icing)

Cream the butter, salt and sugar in bowl of mixer. Add the egg yolks and beat until creamy. Add the orange zest and milk or orange juice. Beat to combine.

Spread on cake.

Oatmeal Cake

(Notebook 11, pp 2)

This is a wonderful moist cake with a great consistency. The broiled topping that contains butter, brown sugar and cocoanut is unique.

Preheat oven to: 350 degrees
Baking pan: 8-by-8-inch baking dish

Ingredients:
(cake)
1 1/4 cups boiling water
1 cup old fashioned oatmeal
1/2 cup butter (one stick)
1 cup brown sugar
1 cup granulated sugar
2 eggs
1/2 tsp cinnamon
1 tsp vanilla
1 1/2 cups flour
1 tsp baking soda
1/2 tsp salt

(topping)
3 tbsp butter, melted
2/3 cups brown sugar
2 beaten egg yokes
2 tbsp cream
1 cup grated cocoanut

Directions:
Pour the boiling water over the oatmeal and let it stand for 20 minutes.
Cream the butter and sugars. Add the eggs and vanilla. Mix well then
add the oats then the remaining ingredients.
Pour into the baking pan and bake 30 minutes at 350 degrees.
Mix all the ingredients for the topping and spread on top of the cake while it is still hot.
Put the cake in the middle of the oven under the broiler one to five minutes, watching it carefully,
until the top browns.

Hot Coffee Chocolate Cake

(*Corps* cookbook pp 148 and Kelchner Notebook #1, pp 143)

This might be Linda's favorite cake. She learned to make when she was 13, which would have been in 1968. The recipe card in our kitchen notebook #1 probably came from Joan about 1996.

According to Linda:

" My mother and grandmother called it 'Linda's Hot Coffee Chocolate Cake' because I made it all the time. It was the first cake I ever learned to make. It was easy. You just put everything in the (mixer) bowl. And, it's chocolate, so what's not to like? My grandmother called it 'Linda's Chocolate Cake' when she put it in the Corps cookbook (pp 148).

Preheat oven to: 350 degrees
Baking Dish: 9-by-13-inch (3 quart) baking dish or two nine-inch layer pans

Ingredients:
2 cups sugar
2 cups flour
1 tsp baking powder
2 tsp baking soda
3/4 cups cocoa
1/2 cup shortening, melted
1 cup hot coffee
1 cup milk
2 eggs
1 tsp vanilla

Directions:
Brew one cup of strong coffee.
Mix the dry ingredients in a mixer bowl. Add liquid ingredients and mix well.
Pour into the nine-by-13 inch baking dish or two nine-inch layer pans.
Bake at 350 degrees for 30-35 minutes.

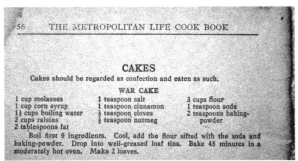

War Cake

(Metropolitan Life 1918 Cookbook, pp 56)

We doubt if Joan ever made this and probably didn't even know she had the recipe for it. It was in a copy of the 1918 Metropolitan Life cookbook that was in her collection of recipes. Given the date, it must have come from Joan's grandmother Susanna Rothenberger, since in 1918 she would have been 43 and Joan's mother Florence only four.

The recipe is an artifact of its time. It contains no milk or eggs and calls for "fat," which probably translated to "anything you can get." It also calls for corn syrup and molasses as sweeteners, a nod to the rationing of sugar in the U.S. as a result of World War One.

The recipe also appears in a charity cookbook *The Educated Palate*, published by the alumnae of Penn Hall Junior College in Chambersburg, Pa., probably in 1973, the year the school closed.

It is one of the first recipes in the book and is titled "Wartime Cake." The ingredients are the same as the Metropolitan Life recipe although some of the quantities are different.

According to the Penn Hall cookbook it was: "A classic cake going back to World War I (when it was called Canadian War Cake), so delicious that ma(n)y homemakers kept it in their repertoire long after rationing ended. An easy recipe from a wartime Better Crocker Booklet called *Your Share.*"

During World War One, rationing of sugar began in mid-1918. In the U.S., civilians were allowed eight ounces per week in order to free up more for U.S. military forces and to help feed hard-pressed U.S. allies in Europe. To make matters worse, the price of rationed goods skyrocketed. Hoarding and a black market emerged. U.S. homemakers began using substitutes like molasses and corn syrup. Since lard, butter and meat were also rationed, Crisco gained in popularity.[46]

Crisco, a hydrogenated vegetable oil sold as a substitute for butter and lard, had been introduced in 1911 by Procter & Gamble.[47]

This really is an interesting cake, unlike anything else. It is very moist and a bit dense, but it has a good gingerbread-like flavor and the raisins add a pleasant texture and flavor.

After you taste it you wonder why cooks didn't continue to make it. It isn't a fast recipe since it calls for the molasses, corn syrup, raisins and seasonings to be brought to a boil then cooled (an investment of at least two hours) before stirring in the flour and leavening agents.

Oven temperature: 375 degrees

Baking pan: two loaf pans

Ingredients:

1 cup molasses

1 cup corn syrup

1 1/2 cups boiling water

2 cups raisins

2 tablespoons fat (use Crisco if you want to try for authenticity)

1 tsp salt

1 tsp cinnamon

1/2 tsp cloves

1/2 tsp nutmeg

3 cups flour

1 tsp baking soda

2 tsp baking powder

Directions:

Bring the first nine ingredients to a boil in a sauce pan. Allow to cool.

Combine the flour, baking soda, baking powder and add to the liquid mixture.

Pour into two greased loaf pans. Bake at 375 degrees for 45 minutes.

My Marble Cake

(Notebook 11, pp 19)

Preheat oven to: 350 degrees
Baking pan: two nine-inch layer pans

Ingredients:
3 cups plus 3 tbsp flour
2 1/4 cup sugar
6 tsp baking powder
1 1/2 tsp salt
1 1/2 cups milk
1 1/2 tsp vanilla
6 large egg whites
3/4 cups Crisco

(for chocolate part)
2 squares baking chocolate
1/4 cup sugar
3 tbsp water

Directions:
Combine flour, sugar, baking powder and salt in mixing bowl. Add Crisco, milk and vanilla, combine. Add egg whites and combine.

Remove half the batter to a bowl.

Combine the baking chocolate, sugar and water in a sauce pan. When melted and well combined, add to the batter in the mixing bowl and combine well.

Divide the white portion of the batter in two nine-inch layer pans. Pour the chocolate batter into the center of the white batter then swirl with a knife or spatula,

Bake at 350 degrees for one hour.

Black Bottom Cake

(Cards #4)

This is an interesting recipe. It's essentially an oil-based chocolate cake with a topping of cream-cheese batter and chocolate chips. What makes it different though is the two tablespoons of vinegar in the batter that cuts the sweetness a bit.

The recipe we have is in Linda's handwriting and came from her collection of recipes. Whenever Linda would ask Joan for one of her recipes, Joan would give her a blank card from her recipe box and very impatiently say: "Here. Copy it!"

Preheat oven to: 350 degrees

Baking pan: 9-by-13-inch (3 quart) baking dish

Ingredients:

(topping batter)

8 oz cream cheese

1 egg

1/2 cup sugar

(cake)

2 cups sugar

2 eggs

2/3 cup vegetable oil

2 tbsp vinegar

2 tsp vanilla

2 cups water

3 cups flour

1/2 cup cocoa

2 tsp baking soda

(top)

6 oz chocolate chips

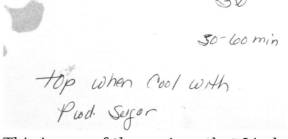

This is one of the recipes that Linda copied. It's on a recipe card that was the dimensions of Joan's recipe box (Box #3). We didn't find the recipe anywhere in Joan's archive.

Directions:

(topping batter)

In a mixer bowl, combine the cream cheese, egg and sugar. Scrape into another bowl and set aside.

(cake batter)

In the mixer bowl, cream the sugar and eggs. Add the oil, vinegar and vanilla and mix thoroughly. Add the water and combine well.

Add the flour, cocoa and baking soda and mix to combine.

Pour the cake batter into a nine-by-13-inch baking pan. Pour the topping batter on top and swirl slightly. Sprinkle the chocolate chips on top.

Bake at 350 degrees for 60-65 minutes.

Jewish Apple Cake

(Cards #2)

I can remember this recipe from the early 1970s. It was unique in that the recipe called for orange juice. It seemed like everybody in our circle of friends (Northeastern and south-central Pennsylvania) was making it. I also recall everyone called it "Jewish Apple Coffee Cake."

Joan got this recipe from Linda (it's in Linda's handwriting) who remembers obtaining it from a co-worker at the Corner House store in Quakertown about 1975-6.

Possibly, it was a recipe that came out of the Southeastern Pennsylvania-New Jersey-Maryland area. I found a similar recipe for a "Jewish Apple Cake" from 1968 in the Baltimore Sun that included orange juice.[48] Also in 1968, the Acme grocery store chain was advertising "Jewish Apple Cake" in papers in Philadelphia.[49] In 1969, the chain was advertising it in Lancaster, Pa.,[50] and Long Branch, N.J.[51]

I found no apple cake recipe in the cookbook *Jewish Cookery*, published in 1949.[52]

It does bear an interesting resemblance to a common Russian cake called sharlotka, which is made with stale bread soaked in milk and egg, with alternate layers of apple and seasoned with sugar and cinnamon. The writers of *Russian Cuisine in Exile (*Boston: Academic Studies Press, 2018,), Pyotr Vail and Alexander Genis, said it was an "ancient Jewish treat."

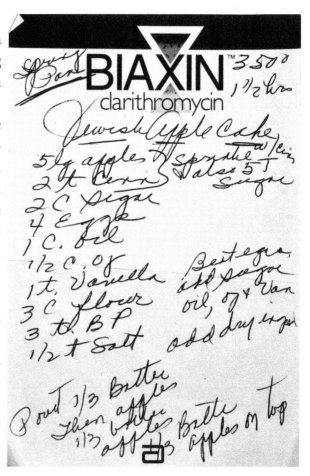

There is an entry in Wikipedia which says it's a Pennsylvania thing and may have originated in Poland.[53]

Preheat oven to: 350 degrees
Baking pan: Bundt pan

Ingredients:
(filling)
5 large apples
5 tbsp sugar
2 tsp cinnamon

(batter)
2 cups sugar
4 eggs
1 cup oil
1/2 cup orange juice

1 tsp vanilla
3 cups flour
3 tsp baking powder
1 tsp salt

Directions:
(for filling)
Peel the apples and slice into eighths. Place in bowl and sprinkle with the five teaspoons of sugar and the cinnamon. Mix well and set aside.

(for the batter)
Beat the eggs, sugar, oil, orange juice and vanilla. Add the dry ingredients and mix to combine.

(to assemble)
Layer in the pan as follows:
-- one third of the batter
-- one third of the apples
-- the second third of the batter
-- the second third of the apples
-- the remaining third of the batter
-- the remaining third of the apples
Bake at 350 degrees for one and one-half hours.

Chocolate Buttermilk Cake

(Kelchner notebook 1, pp 166)

Linda was well familiar with this cake when she was growing up and she copied this recipe from her mother sometime before 1997. That was fortunate because we found no copy of it in Joan's recipes and it's a great cake.

Preheat oven to: 350 degrees

Baking pan: 9-by-13-inch (3 quart) baking dish

Ingredients:

3 cups flour

2 cups sugar

1/2 cup cocoa

2 tsp baking powder

1 tsp baking soda

1 cup (2 sticks) butter at room temperature

Salt

2 eggs, beaten

1 cup buttermilk

1 tsp vanilla

1 cup hot water

Directions:

In a mixer bowl, combine the flour, sugar, cocoa, baking powder, baking soda and salt. Mix slowly to combine well. Add the butter and continue to beat slowly until mostly combined.

Combine the eggs, buttermilk and vanilla. Mix well and add to the dry ingredients in the mixer bowl. Combine then add the hot water.

Pour into a nine-by-13-inch baking pan and bake at 350 degrees for 30-35 minutes.

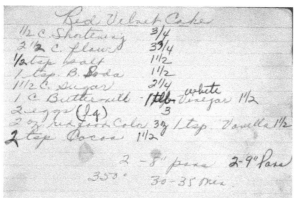

Red Velvet Cake

(Cards #2)

This is an American classic and we found the exact recipe that Joan had, called "Waldorf Red Velvet Cake," in the *Terre Haute Tribune* in April of 1960. It was in a column "Things I see and Hear, by Bea," written by Beatrice Briggs. Briggs said she had gotten the recipe from Mrs. John McAllister (age 72) of West Terre Haute.[54]

In December, 1961, the paper ran the recipe again saying it had received numerous requests for it. The recipe apparently exploded in popularity and appeared in newspapers nationwide about that

(crust and filling)

Wrap the outside of the pan with aluminum foil to catch any liquid that might cook out.

Mix the Graham cracker crumbs, sugar and butter well. Pat them into the sides and bottom of the spring-form pan.

Drain the fruit and spread it in the bottom of the pan.

(filling)

Beat cream cheese until it is smooth then add the eggs one at a time and beat them to combine. Add the sugar and vanilla and beat until smooth.

Pour the batter into the pan over the fruit and bake on a baking sheet 55 minutes at 375 degrees or until the top is light brown. Remove from oven and let set for five minutes. Turn the oven to 450.

(topping)

Beat the sour cream, sugar and vanilla until smooth. Pour over the baked cake. Bake for an additional 10 minutes at 450 degrees then remove from oven.

Allow the cake to cool on rack then refrigerate for at least six hours.

Keep refrigerated.

Black Raspberry Cheesecake

(Notebook 8, pp 6)

Ingredients:
(crust)
1/3 cup chocolate chips
4 tbsp cup butter, melted
1 1/4 cup chocolate graham cracker crumbs

(filling)
5 8-ounce packages of cream cheese
1/2 cup sugar
1/2 cup flour
6 eggs
17 oz black raspberry preserves

(topping)
1/2 cups sour cream
1 1/2 tbsp sugar
1 1/2 tbsp Chambord

Directions:
(Important!) Set out butter, cream cheese, eggs and sour cream for 1-2 hours to come to room temperature.
(crust)
Melt the chocolate chips carefully in a bowl in microwave (heat 20 seconds, stir, repeat until melted). Add butter and stir to melt. Stir in cracker crumbs.

Press into the sides and bottom of a 10-inch spring form pan. Begin with the sides. If there isn't much of the crust material to cover the bottom, brush some off the bottom of the sides with your finger. The bottom crust will be thinner than the sides. This is not a problem.

Put the pan in in the refrigerator and chill for at least an hour.

(filling)
At this point, preheat oven to: 325 degrees
In mixer bowl, cream the cream cheese and sugar. Add the flour and mix thoroughly. Add the eggs, two at a time, mixing thoroughly after each addition.

Add preserves and mix until thoroughly combined.

Pour into the chilled crust.

Bake in 325-degree oven for one hour.

Remove from oven and allow to cool while you make the topping (below) about five minutes.

(topping)
In mixing bowl, thoroughly combine the sour cream, sugar and Chambord.

Pour over top of cheesecake, spread evenly with spatula and return to oven for eight minutes.

Remove from oven and cool on rack until the cake is completely cool, two or three hours, before refrigerating. Do not remove the sides of the spring-form pan until the cheesecake has been chilled thoroughly in the refrigerator.

Placing the cake in the refrigerator while it is still warm could cause it to crack.

Cheesecake Supreme

(Notebook 11, pp 3)

(Important!) Set out butter, cream cheese and eggs for one or two hours to come to room temperature.

Ingredients:
(crust)
1 cup flour
1/4 cup sugar
1 tsp grated lemon zest
1/2 cup butter
1 egg yolk, beaten
1/4 tsp vanilla

(filling)
5 8-oz blocks of cream cheese
3/4 tsp grated lemon zest
1/4 tsp vanilla
1 3/4 cups sugar
3 tbsp flour
1/4 tsp salt
4 eggs
2 egg yolks
1/4 cup heavy cream

(cherry sauce topping)
1 20 oz can of tart cherries
1/2 cup sugar
2 tbsp corn starch.

Directions:
Preheat oven to: 400 degrees

(bottom crust)
Mix flour, sugar and lemon zest in mixer bowl. Add butter and combine thoroughly. Add egg yolk and vanilla and combine.

Press one third of the dough onto the bottom of a nine-inch spring-form pan (sides removed). Bake at 400 degrees for eight minutes. Remove from oven and cool.

(side crust)

Lightly butter the sides of the spring form pan and attach it to the bottom which contains the bottom crust. Press the remaining two-thirds of the dough onto the sides. I found that doing half of it at a time makes it a bit easier.

(filling)

Preheat oven to: 450 degrees.

Put the cream cheese in the mixer bowl and beat it until it's creamy. Add the lemon zest and vanilla and mix.

In another bowl, combine the sugar, flour and salt then gradually add it to the cream cheese mixture in the mixer bowl.

Add eggs and egg yolks, one at a time, beating the mixture after each.

Remove the bowl from the mixer and stir in the heavy cream by hand with a spatula or spoon.

Pour the mixture into the prepared spring-form pan.

Bake at 450 degrees for 12 minutes then reduce the heat to 300 degrees and bake for an additional 55 minutes or until a knife stuck in the middle comes out clean. If it isn't done in 55 minutes, bake for 10 minutes more then check for doneness again.

Remove from oven and cool 30 minutes. The cake will shrink in the middle.

Loosen the side crust with a thin knife. Cool 30 minutes and remove the sides of the spring-form pan. Cool for two hours.

(topping)

Combine the cherries, sugar and corn starch in a sauce pan. Heat, stirring constantly until it comes to a boil and thickens. Simmer 10 minutes, stirring frequently, then pour over top of cheese cake and put the cake in the refrigerator for the topping to cool.

Cheesecake New York Style

(Cards #2)

Linda remembers Joan making this, got the recipe from her and made it as well. It's an interesting cheesecake. It is less sweet and has a unique texture much different than other styles.

Note: it is important that all ingredients be at room temperature

Preheat oven to: 350 degrees

Baking pan: 10-inch springform pan

Ingredients:
Butter to coat the pan
1 cup graham cracker crumbs
3 8-oz packages cream cheese
1 cup sugar
3 tbsp flour
8 oz sour cream
8 oz light cream
6 eggs
1 tsp vanilla

Directions:
Coat the spring-form pan well with butter then shake the graham cracker crumbs on all surfaces to adhere to the butter.

Separate the eggs, put the whites in the bowl of a mixer and whip until stiff. Transfer to a large mixing bowl.

In the empty mixer bowl, add the cream cheese, flour, sour cream, light cream, vanilla and egg yolks. Beat until well combined.

Fold the cheese mixture into the beaten egg whites and pour into prepared spring-form pan.

Place a pan of hot water on the bottom shelf of the heated oven then place the springform pan on a shelf in the middle. Bake for one hour.

Turn off the oven and allow the cheesecake to sit in the hot oven for 15 additional minutes. Open the oven door about four inches and allow the cake to sit for an additional 45 minutes.

Remove cheesecake from oven and refrigerate.

Peanut Butter Cheesecake

(Notebook 8, pp 5)

Preheat oven to: 350 degrees
Pan: 10-inch springform pan

Ingredients:
(bottom crust)
1 1/2 cups salted pretzel crumbs (pulse in food processor)
1/3 cup (2/3 stick) butter, melted

(filling)
5 eight-oz blocks of cream cheese (at room temperature)
1 1/2 cups sugar
3/4 cup creamy peanut butter
3 large eggs
2 tsp vanilla
(icing)
8 oz sour cream
3 tbsp creamy peanut butter
1/2 cup sugar

Directions:
(bottom crust)
Grease the spring-form pan.
Combine the pretzel crumbs and melted butter. Press into the bottom of the spring-form pan. Bake at 350 degrees for 10 minutes.
(filling)
Beat the cream cheese until fluffy.
Gradually add the sugar and peanut butter and continue beating.
Add the eggs one at a time, beating after each one. Add the vanilla, mix thoroughly and pour into the greased spring-form pan.
Bake at 350 degrees for 40 minutes.
Turn off the oven, open the oven door partially and leave the cheese cake in the oven for 30 minutes.
(Icing)
Combine the sour cream, peanut butter and sugar. Spread on warm cheese cake. Chill for eight hours.

15

Pies

Pie has been around for a LOOONG time:

> *Pie makers were familiar features in medieval England. The pie was a development of the Roman idea of using a flour and water paste to seal the cooked juices of a piece of meat. But because in England butter and lard were mixed in with the flour, it was possible to make a free-standing paste container that could be packed full of a mixture of meat, game, fish and vegetables.*[57] – *Cambridge World History of Food*

Rothenberger Family Pie Crust

(Notebook 11, pp 15 and 12, pp 1)

Linda remembers that Joan and her mother Florence both used this crust to make meat pies – beef, chicken and rabbit.

It is a recipe that came down through four generations. Joan's grandmother, Susanne Rothenberger (1875-1950) was the cook of origin for this.

It's a unique recipe (today). It calls for lard to be melted with boiling water, salt then combined with flour. The dough then rests for two hours. Web mentions of similar pie crusts invariably associate it with grandmothers born in the 19th century. The same recipe appears in the 1950 *Pennsylvania State Grange Cook Book*[58] submitted by Mrs. Elva Springer of the Banner Grange No. 1115 in Ebensburg, Cambria County.

Joan's recipe also is essentially a doubling of the "Hot Water Pie Crust" in the first edition of *Joy of Cooking*, which was self-published in 1931 by Irma Rombauer of St. Louis. *Joy of Cooking* went on to become the foremost American cookbook. It has been in print since Bobbs-Merrill first published it in 1936 and has gone through eight editions, all edited by Irma Rombauer's descendants.[59]

Hot-water pie crust isn't used much today in the U.S. It is, however, the traditional dough used to make English pork pies. It was listed among the 2,000 recipes in the highly influential (in England) *Book of Household Management* by Isabella Beeton, published in London in 1861.

It works as directed although it rolls out a bit stiffly. It does hold together and form nicely. The resulting baked crust is very good with a nice consistency.

The first time I tried it, I used it to make apple dumplings. I found that after I wrapped the dough around the apples, I could easily mold it to their shape.

There are five types of fat traditionally used for pie crusts (not oil crusts): lard, butter, margarine, suet and shortening. They can be mixed. A mix of butter and shortening is probably the most common. Suet is not common in the U.S.

Cooks concerned with economy gravitate to margarine and shortening. Those who want the authentic flavor of grandma's recipes choose lard. Bakers who are striving for a certain flakiness pick shortening or butter, or a combination. You can get in long conversations about pie crust with older women at the butcher's counter while you are purchasing lard.

In Linda's recipe box we found a premium cookbook that was intended to draw customers to Dexo shortening. We don't know if Joan used Dexo. If it was economical, she probably did.

Dexo was a private label store brand of shortening sold by the The Great Atlantic and Pacific Tea Company (A&P) chain. Although we couldn't find the dates that it was first and last sold, we did find 10 images of Dexo packaging on the Web with dates between 1940 and 1956. A&P was the largest retail grocery chain in the U.S. for 60 years from 1915-1975. Until 1965 it was the largest retailer of any kind.

Dexo premium cookbook found in Linda's recipe box.
The 16-page booklet contained recipes for desserts and
fried chicken

These "cookbooklets," intended to draw customers to purchase products, date as far back as the Civil War. Although there is no comprehensive list of them, it's been estimated that there are more than 100,000 in collections.[60]

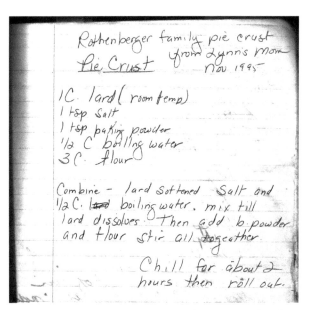

Linda's copy of the recipe, noting that it was a family
recipe — Nov. 1995

Joan's entry—page 1 of her Notebook 12.

It appeared that Joan began copying recipes from elsewhere into Notebook 12, thus her pie crust recipe would be the first entry. The notebook is titled: "Pies + Crusts Puddings and Desserts." It contained a number of loose recipes including three clipped from publications dated Oct 4, 1990; 2004 and August 1, 2005.

Linda also had a copy of the recipe in her recipe file card box (#4) that she used in the 1980s.

Ingredients:
1 cup lard at room temperature
1 tsp salt
1 tsp baking powder
1/2 cup boiling water
3 cups flour

Directions:
Put the lard, salt and boiling water in a mixing bowl. Stir until the lard melts.

Combine the flour and baking powder. Combine the lard-water mixture with the flour. A food processor works very well for this.

Wrap in plastic wrap and refrigerate for at least two hours.

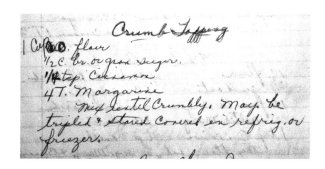

Crumb Topping

This is a seriously important recipe for pies with a crumb topping such as strawberry-rhubarb. We love it because it contains oatmeal, which gives it a wonderful texture and flavor. Linda got it from Joan years ago.

Ingredients:
2/3 cup brown sugar
1/2 cup oatmeal
1/2 cup flour
1/3 cup butter
3/4 tsp cinnamon
1/4 tsp salt

Directions:
Mix ingredients well until they're crumbly.
Sprinkle on top of pie.

My P(eanut) Butter Pie

(Notebook 12, pp 10)

Ingredients:

8 oz cream cheese

14 oz can sweetened condensed milk

1 cup peanut butter

2 tbsp lemon juice

1 tsp vanilla

6 oz Cool Whip (3/4 of an eight ounce container) thawed, which takes about 15 minutes.

Graham cracker crust in nine-inch pie pan

Directions:

In mixer, combine cream cheese and peanut butter. Add condensed milk, lemon juice and vanilla. Beat until well mixed.

Fold in Cool Whip, turn into pie shell, cover with chopped peanuts and refrigerate.

My Pumpkin Pie

(Notebook 11, pp 4)

Preheat oven to: 400 degrees
Baking pan: 9-inch pie pan

Ingredients:
2/3 cup sugar
1 tbsp flour
1/2 tsp salt
1/2 tsp nutmeg
1 tsp cinnamon
1/8 tsp cloves
2 eggs
1/3 cup molasses
2 cups pumpkin
1 cup evaporated milk

Directions:
Combine the sugar, flour and seasonings and mix well.
Add remaining ingredients and stir to combine. Pour into a nine-inch pie crust.
Bake at 400 degrees for 40 minutes.

Apple and Pumpkin Pie

(Notebook 12, pp 3)

Linda and her son Michael (Joan's grandson) both love this. It is expected at all Thanksgiving and Christmas dinners.

It's a really unique recipe calling for apples to be baked into a pumpkin pie which is seasoned with cinnamon and, of all things, pepper.

Preheat oven to: 375 degrees
Baking Pan: 9-inch pie pan

Ingredients:
1 21-oz can apple pie filling
1 1/4 cups pumpkin
2 eggs
1/2 cup brown sugar, packed
3/4 cup half and half
3/4 tsp cinnamon
1/4 tsp black pepper
1/8 tsp salt

Directions:
Line a nine-inch pie pan with crust.
Pour apple pie filling into crust. Mix remaining ingredients and pour over apples.
Bake 375 degrees for 60 minutes.

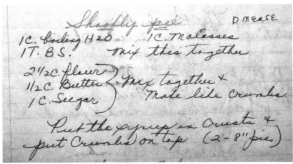

Shoo fly pie

(Notebook 11, pp 24 and *Corps*, pp 99)

If someone knows one thing about the Pennsylvania Dutch it's that they eat shoo fly pie. The pies are advertised to tourists and served in diners in Lancaster County and throughout eastern Pennsylvania.

Pennsylvania food historian William Woys Weaver has detailed the history of the Pennsylvania Dutch in his excellent book *As American as Shoofly Pie, The Folklore and Fakelore of Pennsylvania Dutch Cuisine.*[61]

The Pennsylvania Dutch are people descended from immigrants who came from areas that became Germany, France and Switzerland. In the 18th century when these people were immigrating to Pennsylvania, they were called the Dutch: "low" Dutch came from the lower Rhine river in and near the Netherlands, and the "high" Dutch from the southern Rhineland, Swabia and Switzerland. The country of Germany didn't come into existence until 1872. William Shakespeare (1564-1616) called German-speaking people "Dutchmen."

The language called "Pennsylvania Dutch," is descended from a dialect of German called West Central German, that came from the Rhine region of Germany with immigrants in the 18th century. About 400,000 people still speak it in the U.S. and Canada and about a million Germans speak something similar to the original dialect in the Rhineland.

Most people assume that the Pennsylvania Dutch are Amish. That is a result of 100 years of "fakelore" produced by fiction writers and the tourist industry, according to Weaver. Some of the Pennsylvania Dutch are Lutherans, Mennonites and even Swiss Catholics. To add to the confusion, Swiss Brethren and Schwenkfelder people who settled in the area around Bethlehem (not far from Quakertown) are often called "Dutch" as well. Joan had a Schwenkfelder church charity cookbook in her collection.

The Pennsylvania Dutch people were not all famers nor did they all live in the country. Some lived in towns and cities like Reading, Allentown, Harrisburg and Chambersburg, according to Weaver. Some were poor (the "buckwheat" Dutch) and some were middle class or wealthy (the Hasenpfeffer Dutch).

Linda and I both are descended from Pennsylvania Dutch immigrants (mine from the Palatinate and hers from Switzerland). We grew up eating shoo fly pie and everyone we knew ate it. It was at every family reunion and church supper.

It's a pie made with a liquid molasses base covered with crumbs made of butter, flour and brown sugar. When baked it can be more liquid (wet bottom) or dryer and cake-like (dry bottom).

Where it came from is a bit of a mystery. Pennsylvania food historian William Woys Weaver believes it descended from a Centennial Cake that was originally created at the 1876 Centennial celebration in Philadelphia. Sometime after the Civil War, Pennsylvania Dutch cooks began using English style pie crusts made with butter or lard, which became common then. After the Centennial, somebody apparently got the idea of making the Centennial Cake in a pie form. The recipe circulated among country cooks in Pennsylvania afterward, sometimes being called "Granger" pie.[62] "Shoo Fly" refers to the brand of molasses that was often used to make it.

Weaver said his grandmother got a "Centennial pie" recipe from a friend in Ephrata, Pa., in the early 30s.[63]

There is a recipe for Centennial Cake in the *The Heirloom Cookbook* (published by the Quakertown Historic Society), which was in Joan's collection, but it bears no resemblance at all to shoo fly cake or pie. It's baked in a loaf pan and contains dried fruit.[64]

Boston-based food historian Mark H. Zanger, writing in the *Oxford Encyclopedia of Food and Drink in America,* said a "shoo fly cake" recipe appeared in a manuscript from Pennsylvania in 1890. He wrote that "shoo fly cake" and "shoo fly pie" appeared in a church charity cookbook from Mount Carmel, Pa, about the same time -- *The Talent Cookbook*, published by the Grace Evangelical Lutheran Church.

Zanger said he found one shoo fly pie recipe in a 1915 collection from Reading, Pa., and another from 1916 called "German shoo fly."[65]

The recipe we have from Joan's collection, which we have used since the early 1990s, was contributed to the *Corps* cookbook by Joan's aunt Estella.

Note: The recipe calls for a crumb topping and a liquid base. A pie shell full of molasses-colored water with crumbs on top seems quite alarming. Trust the recipe. It works.

When you pour the liquid into the pie shell it can easily splash over the sides. It's a good idea to place your pie pan on a baking sheet to assemble the pie and bake it.

Preheat oven to: 450 degrees
Baking dish: 9-inch pie pan

Ingredients:
(crumbs)
1 cup flour
3/4 cup brown sugar
2 tbsp butter

(bottom)
1 egg, beaten
1 cup molasses
3/4 cup hot water
1 tsp baking soda
pinch of salt

Directions:
(for crumbs)
Mix the flour, brown sugar and butter well with a fork, forming crumbs. Set aside.

(for liquid)
Combine the egg, molasses, water, salt and baking soda.

(to assemble)
Carefully pour the liquid into a nine-inch pie shell. Sprinkle the crumbs evenly on top.
Bake at 450 degrees for five minutes then lower the oven to 375 and bake for 45 minutes.

Funny Cake

(Cards #2 and #4 and Notebook 11, pp 24)

Funny Cake, a sort of chocolate version of shoo fly pie, has been a family favorite through at least four generations. It was one of the first recipes that Lin copied into our kitchen notebook when we first got together in 1992. She copied the recipe from Joan's notebook version too because it was missing the baking time and temperature, which were on the file card in recipe file box #2.

Linda remembered funny cake, and had her own idea about where it got its name:

" You'd pour the chocolate on the top and it would end up on the bottom. It was funny. That's what I thought.

It was my favorite pie when I was 10 or 11. My granny Scheetz would make them and bring them over because she knew I liked them

Joan had gotten the recipe from her mother-in-law Minnie (Gassmeir) Scheetz of Quakertown. Minnie and Joan had worked together, been friends and socialized. Minnie's son Kenneth was serving in the Navy and Minnie introduced him and Joan. Ken and Joan were married in 1955.

Preheat oven to: 350 degrees
Baking pan: 9-inch pie pan

Ingredients:
(cake batter)
1 1/4 cups flour
1 tsp baking powder
1/2 tsp salt
3/4 cups sugar
1/4 cup shortening or lard, melted
1/2 cups milk
1 tsp vanilla
1 egg

(sauce)
1 square baking chocolate
1/4 cup water
2/3 cup sugar
1/4 cup butter
1 tsp vanilla

Directions:
Have a pie shell ready.
(For sauce)
Combine baking chocolate and water in a saucepan. Stir over low heat until the chocolate is all melted.

Add the sugar and butter and bring to a boil. Remove from heat and stir in vanilla. Set aside, off heat, until the cake is assembled

(for cake)

In the bowl of the mixer, combine flour, baking powder, salt and sugar.

In a separate bowl, combine the milk, melted shortening or butter, vanilla and beaten egg. Add the wet ingredients to the dry ingredients in the mixer bowl and beat well.

(to assemble)

Pour half the chocolate sauce into a pie shell. Pour in the batter then top with the remaining sauce.

Bake at 350 degrees for 45-55 minutes.

Strawberry Rhubarb Pie

(Notebook 11, pp 8)

This is Linda's father, Ken Sheetz senior's, favorite pie and she makes one for him every time he visits when there is rhubarb in the garden.

Rhubarb has been used by man for 5,000 years. It was native to southern Siberia and China and has been cultivated in Europe at least since the 17th century.[66]

On these shores, it was first planted in Maine when a farmer obtained some seeds from Europe shortly after the American Revolution. It soon spread throughout the U.S. and by the 1830s was popular for pies, cobblers, conserves and tarts. Rhubarb extract and syrup also were a standard treatment for stomach and bowel complaints throughout the 19th century.[67]

Ingredients:
1 1/4 cup sugar
1/8 tsp salt
1/3 cup flour
2 cups fresh strawberries, sliced 1/4 inch thick
1 cup rhubarb cut in one-inch pieces
2 tbsp butter
1 tbsp sugar (if using top crust)

Directions:
Combine the sugar, salt and flour in a bowl. Add the sliced strawberries and rhubarb pieces. Allow to stand for 15 minutes, stirring occasionally.

Pour into a pie shell and cover with top pastry or crumb topping.

For covered pie: bake 425 degrees for 40-50 minutes, until the top is slightly browned.

For pies with crumb topping, bake at 400 degrees for five minutes, then reduce the oven to 350 and bake and additional 50 minutes.

Mince Meat

(Cards #2)

Joan got this recipe from Anna Knechel, her second husband, Donald's, mother. It may be Anna's handwriting on the card, it isn't Joan's.

According to Linda:

" *My mother said it was the best mincemeat she ever ate. My step father loved mincemeat pie.* *"*

Mincemeat pies are considered English and have a history going far back. According to Larousse Gastronomique:

" *In the 17th century, a mince pie was a huge covered tart filled with ox (beef) tongue, chicken,* *"* *eggs, sugar, raisins, lemon zest and spices. Gradually the small tartlets replaced the single large tart and the filing was reduced to a mixture of beef, suet, spices and dried fruit, steeped in brandy.[68]*

Larousse Gastronomique, considered the ultimate reference on food, was originally written by Prosper Montagné (1864-1948) in 1938 and has been updated ever since. Montagné was a notable 19th century French chef and writer. In the 1920s his Paris restaurant Rue de l'Échelle was considered the best in France.[69]

Amelia Simmons included a recipe for "Minced pie of beef" in her cookbook which is considered to be the first one written in the United States (1796).[70]

Ingredients:
6 pounds beef neck meat or chuck roast
2 pounds raisins
1 pound currents
1 pound brown sugar
2 tsp cinnamon
1 tsp cloves
6 pounds finely chopped apples
24 oz whiskey

Directions:
Cook the meat in a large kettle until a fork goes through it easily. Cool and cut off any fat or gristle. Chop the meat fine in a food processor. Strain the cooking liquid.

Put in a large kettle with other ingredients (except the whiskey) and enough of the cooking liquid to make the mixture moist but not mushy. Cook 10-15 minutes.

Put one third cup of whiskey in each of eight-quart canning jars, fill with mincemeat, seal and water-bath can for 25 minutes.

Canned mincemeat improves with aging. Two or three months is the time usually given.

Joan's cookies (clockwise from top) Peanut Butter Temptations, Anise Cookies, Cocoa Kisses, Peanut Butter Cookies, Potato Chip Cookies, Chocolate Drops with Non Pareils. Chocolate Chip and Oatmeal Cookies and (center) Orange Macadamia Nut Cookies.

16

Cookies

At Christmas there were always mountains of cookies on counters and tables at Joan's home. She had an eye for unique recipes and many became family favorites. "She was into trying different cookies there for a while," Linda said. "She'd make cookies for the kids over there (the townhouse in Quakertown) and put them in baggies with ribbons and they knew it."

Linda did not remember Joan making cookies other times of the year. She'd begin on Halloween – baking cookies to give to trick-or-treaters – and continue through the Thanksgiving and Christmas holiday seasons.

Joan rolled cookies small in order to make a lot of them, so they lasted longer. As a teenager, Linda would be drafted to help make them. She always rolled them too large in order to get finished sooner with the minimum amount of work. This did not make Joan happy. In later years, when Linda started to LIKE making cookies, she discovered that a secret to making lighter cookies that rise properly is to bring the butter and eggs to room temperature before mixing the cookie dough.

The recipe from Joan's notebook 10:

Anise Cookies

(Notebook 10, pp 3, and Cards #1)

We believe that Joan got this recipe from her mother Florence since we found the identical recipe in Florence's recipe box (#1).

Linda remembered them from childhood and loved them.

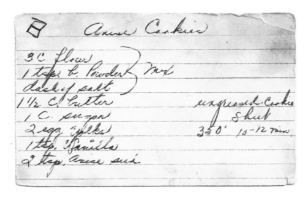

The recipe from Florence's recipe box

Preheat oven to: 350 degrees

Ingredients:
(**Note:** allow the butter and eggs to come to room temperature before mixing the dough.)
3 cups flour
1 tsp baking powder
1/4 tsp salt
2 tsp anise seed
1 1/2 cups butter
1 cup sugar
2 egg yokes
1 tsp vanilla

Directions:
Mix the dry ingredients and set aside.

Cream the butter and sugar with a mixer. Add the yokes and vanilla and mix well. Add the dry ingredients and mix.

Roll into one-inch balls and place on ungreased baking sheet with plenty of room for them to spread. Flatten the balls with the bottom of a small glass. Dip the glass in water if it sticks to the cookies.

Bake in 350-degree oven for 10-12 minutes.

Peanut Butter Cookies

(Notebook 10, pp 15)

We have pretty good evidence that Joan got this recipe from her mother. The title in her notebook entry is "P. Butter Cookies — Mother."

In our photo above, the cookies have been dipped in chocolate. That is not in the original recipe. It's an addition that Linda made.

The secret to melting chocolate chips for coating cookies is to melt them in a bowl in a microwave oven for 20 seconds, stirring the warming chips, then putting them back in the microwave for 20 more seconds and stirring, until the chocolate is melted and liquid enough to coat the cookies.

DO NOT overheat them or try to melt milk chocolate in a double boiler on the stove (in spite of instructions to do so in most cookbooks), it very quickly overheats the chocolate.

Milk chocolate must be heated very carefully. The melting temperature of dark chocolate is between 113 and 122 degrees Fh. (depending on the brand), milk chocolate 104-113 and white chocolate 104 degrees.[71] Heating it above those temperatures causes it to form a crystalized lump that is unusable until it cools and is gently reheated, a process that takes at least an hour.

Preheat oven to: 375 degrees

Ingredients:
1 1/4 cup flour
1/2 tsp salt
1 tsp baking powder
1/2 cup butter
1/2 cup peanut butter
1/2 cup white sugar
1/2 cup brown sugar
1 egg
1/2 tsp vanilla

Directions:
Mix the dry ingredients well — the flour, salt and baking powder — and set aside.

Cream the butter and peanut butter with a mixer. Add the white and brown sugar, vanilla and egg. Beat until light.

Add the dry ingredients and mix thoroughly.

Roll into one-and-one-quarter-inch balls and arrange on a greased baking sheet with plenty of room for the cookies to expand. Flatten the balls with a fork.

Bake in 375-degree oven for 10-12 minutes.

Old Fashioned Peanut Butter Cookies

(Notebook 10, pp 14)

Peanut butter cookies go back more than 100 years. Peanut butter became a vegetarian fad after health food advocate John Harvey Kellogg endorsed in as a substitute for "cow butter" about 1890.[72]

Peanut butter was introduced to mainstream Americans at the 1904 World's Fair in St. Louis, Mo. Manufacturers of the product soon began sponsoring cookbooks with recipes for peanut butter-flavored cookies, with little peanut butter in them compared to today's recipes.

A recipe with more peanut butter appeared in a 1937 cookbook written by Ruth Wakefield of Whitman, Massachusetts, creator of the Toll House cookie.[73]

Joan's recipe is probably pretty close to that one.

There was no peanut butter cookie recipe in the first edition *Joy of Cooking* in 1931, and the "Peanut Drop Cookies" recipe in the first edition of the *Better Homes and Gardens Cookbook* (1930) (pp 15) bears no resemblance to Joan's.

Peanuts have been around for a long time. Indians in Peru were cultivating them 2,000 B.C.E. After Europeans reached the New World, the Spanish took them to the Philippines and the Portuguese took them to Africa. They reached the U.S. with the slave trade and were used commonly as cattle feed.

The distinguished agricultural scientist George Washington Carver, working at the Tuskegee Institute in Alabama, found over 100 uses for them, but he did not invent peanut butter as many think. Southerners ate them during the food shortages of the Civil War caused by Union blockades of their ports and Union soldiers ate them while serving in the southern states during that war. As a consequence, roast peanuts became popular at fairs throughout the country after the Civil War.[74]

Do not preheat oven. Cookie dough must chill for two hours before baking.

Ingredients:
2 1/2 cups flour
1 tsp baking powder
1 tsp baking soda
1/4 tsp salt
1 cup butter
1 cup peanut butter
2 eggs
1 tsp vanilla
1 cup granulated sugar
1 cup brown sugar

Directions:
Combine flour, baking powder, baking soda and salt and set aside.

Combine butter and peanut butter in mixer bowl and beat until combined. Add eggs and vanilla and mix well.

Add granulated and brown sugar and beat until combined. Add flour mixture that had been set aside and beat until well combined.

Chill in refrigerator for two hours.

Roll into balls about one and one-half inches in diameter, place on ungreased baking sheet and flatten slightly with a fork.

Bake 350 degrees for nine minutes — 11 minutes for firmer, crunchier cookies.

Peanut Butter Temptations

(Notebook 10, pp 11)

These have been a Christmas tradition around our house for quite a while. They are among my favorites of Joan's cookie recipes. I found the same recipe in one of our notebooks from 2006. Apparently Joan gave the recipe to Linda.

Preheat oven to: 350 degrees

Ingredients:
1/2 cup butter
1/2 cup peanut butter
1/2 cup granulated sugar
1/2 cup brown sugar
1 egg
½ tsp vanilla
1 1/2 cups flour
3/4 tsp baking soda
1/2 tsp salt

Directions:
In mixer bowl, cream the butter, peanut butter, white sugar and brown sugar.
Add the egg and vanilla and beat well.
Blend the flour, baking soda and salt and add to the mixer bowl. Beat well.
Shape into one-inch balls and place in the indentations of well-greased mini muffin tins. This recipe makes at least 36 cookies.
Bake at 350 degrees for 10-12 minutes.
Remove finished cookies from oven and press a mini peanut butter cup into the center of each. Allow to cool three or four minutes. To remove the cookies from the muffin tin, insert a thin knife down the side of each cookie and slide along edge of the indentation until the cookie moves freely. Carefully lift one side until you can slide the knife beneath and pick the cookie out. Cool on a rack.

Peanut Butter Thumbprints

(Notebook 10, pp 13)

Ingredients:
1 cup butter, softened
2 cups light brown sugar
1 1/2 cups peanut butter
2 eggs
1 tsp vanilla
2 1/2 cups flour
1 tsp baking soda
1 tsp baking powder
1 3/4 cups finely chopped peanuts

(for filling)
3 oz cream cheese
3 tbsp light corn syrup
1/2 tsp vanilla
1 cup chocolate chips, melted
1/2 cup powdered sugar

Directions:
(cookies)
Beat together the butter, brown sugar and peanut butter. Add the eggs and vanilla and combine well. Add the flour, baking powder and baking soda and combine well.

Roll the dough into one-inch balls, roll in the chopped peanuts and arrange on baking sheets. Bake at 350 degrees for 10-12 minutes, until the cookies are just set. Remove from oven and press your thumb into each one to make an indentation. Cool.

(Filling)
Combine with a mixer the cream cheese, corn syrup and vanilla. Add the melted chocolate chips and combine well. Add the powdered sugar and combine until smooth.

Spoon one-half teaspoon of filling into the indentation in each cookie.

(**Note:** to melt chocolate chips, put them in a bowl and microwave for 20 second intervals. Remove and stir to melt the remaining lumps with the heat in the melted chocolate. If needed, microwave a second time for 20 seconds and continue stirring. Do not overheat the chocolate or it will crystalize.)

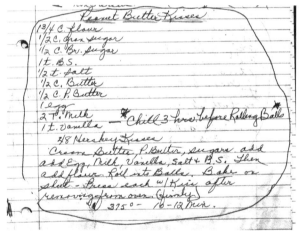

Peanut Butter Kisses

(Notebook 10, pp 7)

Ingredients:
1/2 cup butter
1/2 cup peanut butter
1/2 cup granulated sugar
1/2 cup brown sugar

1 egg
2 tbsp milk
1 tsp vanilla
1/2 tsp salt
1 tsp baking soda
1 3/4 cups flour
48 Hershey Kisses

Directions:

In mixer bowl, cream the butter, peanut butter and sugars.

Add the egg, milk, vanilla, salt and baking soda and combine well.

Add the flour and combine.

Chill the dough in the refrigerator for three hours.

To bake:

Roll into 48 balls and arrange on baking sheets. Bake at 375 degrees for 10-12 minutes.

Remove from oven and press a Hershey Kiss into the center of each cookie. Allow to cool on the baking sheets.

Potato Chip Cookies

(Notebook 10, pp 1 and 18)

These cookies are unique (although there are a lot of recipes for them on the Web) and Linda remembered that Joan loved them. Joan apparently found the recipe somewhere after Linda left home about 1975. She probably copied it into Notebook 10 — on page 1 — from an earlier source. It contains the note "(Excellent)."

We found the recipe twice in Florence's recipe box: once with the title: "Potatoe Chip Cookie Joan" and second time titled: "Potato Chip Cookies (workbasket.)"

The first is identical to the recipe in Joan's notebook, except Joan's calls for one third cup of nuts and Florence's calls for one half cup. We think Joan had an earlier recipe which she gave to her mother then revised it before she copied it into her notebook 10.

Florence's *Workbasket* (magazine) recipe is a completely different recipe. "Potato" is spelled correctly, it would make many more cookies and it calls for a six-ounce package of butterscotch chips. Joan had this same recipe too in Notebook 10, pp 18.

Preheat oven to: 375 degrees

Ingredients:
1 cup butter, softened
1/2 cup granulated sugar
1 tsp vanilla
1/2 cups crushed potato chips
1/3 cup chopped nuts (slivered almonds)
2 cups flour

Directions:
Cream the butter, sugar and vanilla. Add the chips and nuts and mix. Stir in flour.

Form into one-inch balls, roll in sugar and place on baking sheet with room to expand. Flatten slightly with a fork.

Bake at 375 for 15-16 minutes.

Orange Macadamia Nut Cookies

(Notebook 10, pp 2)

Everybody in the family seems to remember these. They were around every Christmas season and could be expected on Joan's kitchen counter throughout the holidays.

Preheat oven to: 350 degrees

Ingredients:
(Cookies)
4 cups flour
2 cups 10X sugar
1 cup cornstarch
2 cups butter (at room temperature)
1 cup macadamia nuts or toasted walnuts
2 egg yolks at room temperature
1 tbsp orange peel, zested or finely shredded
4-6 tbsp orange juice
granulated sugar

(icing)
2 cups 10X sugar
3 tbsp butter (softened)
1 tbsp grated orange peel
2 tbsp orange juice (add an additional tablespoon of juice if needed)

Directions:
Mix flour, sugar and corn starch and cut in butter until you get a crumbly constancy. Stir in nuts.

Combine yolks, orange peel and four tablespoons of orange juice. Mix well then combine with flour-sugar mixture and knead, adding as much as two tablespoons of orange juice if too dry.

Roll into balls one and one-fourth inches in diameter and arrange on baking sheet with room to expand. Dip a small glass in granulated sugar and flatten each ball until it is about one fourth inch thick.

Bake in 350-degree oven for 25 minutes, or until edges begin to brown.

Remove from oven and cool.

Combine icing ingredients until it reaches a spreadable constancy and spread on cookies.

Makes 55 cookies.

Chocolate Chip and Oatmeal Cookies

(Notebook 10, pp 33)

We know where this recipe came from. We gave it to her. I remembered having the cookies at the Philadelphia restaurant "Frog" probably sometime in the 1980s. Wherever we got the recipe, we copied it in our kitchen notebook in 1993. It's nearly the same as the recipe for "Oatmeal Chocolate Chip Walnut Cookies" in the *Frog Commissary Cookbook*.[75]

Frog was in business from 1973-87 on South 16th Street then the 1500 block of Locust Street A companion restaurant, Commissary, closed in 1994 when owner Steve Poses chose to concentrate his efforts on his Frog Commissary catering business (est. 1975) which is the in-house caterer for the Franklin Institute in Philadelphia.[76]

The recipe, called "Chocolate Chip Oatmeal Cookies (Soft)" appears in the 1978 *Great Radio Cook Book* (pp 131), a charity cookbook published by radio station WLSH in Lansford, in Carbon County. It was submitted by Helen Andrews of Frackville.

A very similar recipe is printed on the packaging for Nestle's Semi-Sweet Morsels at this writing (2018).

The ancestor of these cookies, of course, was the original "Toll House" cookie, America's most popular homemade cookie. It was created by Ruth Wakefield, owner of the Toll House Inn, in Whitman, Mass., in the 1930s. Wakefield's original recipe called for a Nestlé semi-sweet chocolate bar to be chopped into small pieces before being mixed in with the cookie dough. The Nestlé company noticed its regional popularity and in 1939 the company began selling semi-sweet chocolate morsels. Nestlé then got permission from Wekefield to print her recipe on their packages.[77]

Preheat oven to: 350 degrees

Ingredients:
1 cup butter (at room temperature)
1 cup brown sugar (firmly packed)
1 cup granulated sugar
2 tbsp milk
2 eggs beaten (at room temperature)
2 tsp vanilla
2 cups flour
2 1/2 cups old fashioned oatmeal
1 tsp salt
1 tsp baking soda
1 tsp baking powder
1 1/2 cups chopped walnuts
12 oz chocolate chips

Directions:
Cream the butter and sugars Add the milk, eggs and vanilla and combine.
Add dry ingredients (except the nuts and chocolate chips) and mix.
Fold in the nuts and chocolate chips.
Chill for two hours.
Drop about three tablespoons at a time on a baking sheet and bake at 350 degrees for eight or nine minutes.

Chewy Chocolate Chip Cookies

(Notebook 9, pp 2)

I remember Joan making these, generally at holidays. They're a really interesting take on the chocolate chip cookie. They're chocolate, chocolate chip cookies, and if you're a fan of chocolate, it doesn't get any better than that.

They are intended to be soft and chewy rather than crisp, so keep that in mind if you need to adjust the baking time.

Preheat oven to: 350 degrees

Ingredients:
1/2 cup butter at room temperature
1 cup granulated sugar
1/2 cup brown sugar, packed tightly
2 eggs
1 tsp vanilla
2 cups flour
1/3 cup cocoa
1 tsp baking soda
1 tsp salt
12 oz semi-sweet chocolate chips, or 10 oz peanut butter chips

Directions:
Put butter, white and brown sugar in mixer bowl and combine well.
Add the eggs and mix well.
Add vanilla, flour, cocoa, baking soda and salt and combine well.
Fold in the chocolate chips.
Drop by tablespoonful onto greased baking sheet leaving at least two inches between cookies.
Bake at 350 degrees for 10 minutes.

Cooky Quickies

(Notebook 10)

This recipe is a real mystery. The original card was loose in one of Joan's notebooks. It was written in pencil and is so faint that it isn't readable at all. I scanned it into a file and adjusted the contrast until the text stood out enough to read.

The handwriting isn't familiar and neither is the misspelling of the word "cooky." We found other spelling errors in the recipes of Joan's mother Florence, so, she would be a logical source. I found no similar recipe on the Internet. It vaguely resembles the famous no-bake chocolate oatmeal cookies but uses chocolate chips instead of cocoa, butter and sugar, and substitutes corn flakes for the oatmeal.

After I made a batch, Linda remembered Joan making them. Joan bought corn flakes to cook and bake with. Linda also said that she made them for her own children in the 1980s.

There is a vaguely similar recipe in the *Corps* cookbook (pp 169) for "No-bake Peanut Butter Chip Cookies" that calls for peanut butter chips rather than chocolate chips. It also includes raisins.

Ingredients:
6 oz chocolate chips
1/3 cup peanut butter
3 cups corn flakes

Directions:
Melt chocolate chips and peanut butter in bowl in microwave in 20-second intervals. Stirring after each heating.

It is important that you do not overheat the milk chocolate or it will harden into a crystalline mass and be unusable until it is chilled thoroughly and re-melted.

It will take about two minutes before the ingredients are thoroughly melted.

Stir in corn flakes and drop by spoonful onto wax paper. Let cool.

No Bake Oatmeal Cookies

(Notebook 10, pp 30)

The photo above shows a scene that was very familiar in the 1960s and 70s in the homes where Linda and I grew up. No-bake Chocolate Oatmeal Cookies were popular with moms who could make them quickly and with us kids who ate them as quickly as they were made.

We'd lost contact with any recipe for these for many years and strangely, I found one in 1997, lying on the attic floor just one day after it entered my mind to go looking for a recipe. What we found may have been from my first wife's great aunt Alma of Beach Haven in Luzerne County. My first wife inherited Alma's recipe folder with about 100 recipes — all but one of them for cakes, cookies and other desserts. Alma was famous in the family for her baking.

Joan had three recipes for these, two in Notebook 10 and one in her recipe card box #4. The written directions are actually my own personal recipe, which doesn't vary much from Joan's.

I've made these often and have found that one needs to be oddly precise, especially in measuring the milk and in boiling the sugar, cocoa and milk, which must be no less than two minutes.

Ingredients:
1/2 cup butter (1 stick)
1 3/4 cups sugar
1/2 cup cocoa
1/2 cup milk
1 tsp vanilla
1 tbsp peanut butter
3/4 cups raisins (optional)
3 cups old-fashioned oatmeal (uncooked)

Directions:
Place the raisins in a microwave proof container with water to cover. Bring to a boil in the microwave, then drain and set aside.

Melt butter in a large sauce pan.

Add sugar, cocoa and milk. Bring to rolling boil and boil, stirring constantly, for exactly two minutes. This is important. Boiling the ingredients for less than two minutes results in cookies that remain sticky.

Remove pan from heat and stir in the vanilla, peanut butter and raisins (if using) and oatmeal.

Drop from a tablespoon onto wax paper on a counter and cool.

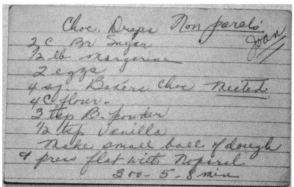

Chocolate Drops with Non Pareils

(Notebook 10, pp 7 and 8; Cards #1 and #4)

This appears to be a recipe with a history. There is a card in Florence's card file box titled "chocolate drops." It is written in pencil and in a hand that is not familiar to us, possible it was written by Joan's grandmother Suzanna. It calls for shortening, nuts and raisins.

The recipe we have reproduced here also was in Florence's card box titled "Chocolate Drops Non Parels (sic) Joan." According to Linda, Joan got it from her childhood friend Mae Wolfinger of Quakertown. Joan had the same recipe in her notebook 10 but with expanded directions for mixing and a hotter oven temperature (350 degrees, up from 300 degrees).

Linda had a copy in her recipe box and she copied the same recipe in our notebook number one (pp 159) about 1996. She has made these for many years, but when I made them they came out softer, possibly because I used the lower oven temperature.

Preheat oven to: 350 degrees

Ingredients:
1/4 pound (one stick) butter
2 oz unsweetened baking chocolate, chopped coarsely
1 cup brown sugar
1/4 tsp vanilla
1 egg
2 cups flour
11/2 tsp baking powder
Nonpareils

Directions:
Carefully melt the butter and baking chocolate in a bowl in the microwave. Heat for 20 seconds, then stir. Heat for a second 20 seconds and stir. Do not overheat.

Transfer to the bowl of a mixer and add the sugar, vanilla and egg. Mix well.

Add the flour and baking powder and mix for 30 seconds or until well combined.

Pick out small amounts of the dough, roll into one-and-one-half-inch balls and arrange on baking sheets with room to expand. Press a nonpareil into the top of each ball, slightly flattening it.

Bake at 350 degrees for 12-15 minutes.

Makes 30 cookies.

M & M Chocolate Chip Cookies

(Notebook 10, pp 6 and Cards #1)

These were "kid" cookies. Joan made them at Halloween to pass out to trick-or-treaters in that far-off age when baked goods were an acceptable (and non-threatening) Halloween treat.

This recipe might go a long way back (1940s, 50s?) We found a similar recipe in file card box #1 which we believe originally belonged to Joan's mother Florence.

M&Ms were first created in the United States by Mars, Inc. in 1941 and were similar to a British candy called "Smarties" that were sold in the 1930s.

Preheat oven to: 350 degrees

Ingredients
2 cups flour
3/4 tsp baking soda
3/4 tsp salt
3/4 cup butter (one and one half sticks, softened to room temperature)
2/3 cups granulated sugar
1/2 cup brown sugar
2 eggs (at room temperature)
1 tsp vanilla
1 3/4 cups (12 oz) M&Ms
3/4 cups chopped walnuts (or other nut)

Directions:
Combine flour, baking soda and salt and set aside.

Cream butter and sugars with mixer then add vanilla and eggs. Beat thoroughly. Add flour mixture and beat thoroughly.

Fold in nuts and M&Ms.

Form into one-and-one-half-inch balls on greased baking sheet, leaving room for cookies to double in size.

Bake at 350 degrees for 12 to 14 minutes.

Malted Milk Ball Cookies

Linda remembered these cookies distinctly and liked them a lot. We found no recipe for them in Joan's records, so we simply took the M&M cookie recipe and substituted the malted milk balls for the M&Ms.

Preheat oven to: 350 degrees

Ingredients
2 cups flour
3/4 tsp baking soda
3/4 tsp salt
3/4 cup butter (one and one-half sticks, softened to room temperature)
2/3 cups granulated sugar
1/2 brown sugar
2 eggs (at room temperature)
1 tsp vanilla
1 3/4 cups malted milk balls cut in half or quarters
3/4 cups chopped walnuts (or other nut)

Directions:
Combine flour, baking soda and salt and set aside.

Cream butter and sugars with mixer then add vanilla and eggs. Beat thoroughly. Add flour mixture and beat thoroughly.

Fold in nuts and malted milk balls.

Form into one-and-one-half-inch balls on greased baking sheet, leaving room for cookies to double in size.

Bake at 350 degrees for 12 to 14 minutes.

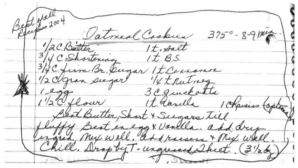

Oatmeal cookies

(Notebook 10, pp 36)

Linda remembers helping Joan make these and, as usual, was scolded for rolling the balls of dough too large. Joan preferred to bake a lot of smaller cookies in the belief that her ravenous sons would eat fewer of them.

Joan's granddaughter Taylor Sheetz also remembered these and ask us to dig out the recipe.

Preheat oven to: 375 degrees

Ingredients:

1/2 cups butter

3/4 cups shortening
3/4 cup brown sugar
1/2 cups granulated sugar
1 egg
1 tsp vanilla
1 1/2 cups flour.
1 tsp salt
1 tsp baking soda
1 tsp cinnamon
1/4 tsp nutmeg
3 cups quick oats
1 cup raisins

Directions:
Put butter, shortening, brown sugar and white sugar in mixer bowl and mix until well fluffy.
Beat in egg and vanilla.
Add flour, salt, baking soda, cinnamon and nutmeg. Run mixer to combine.
Add the oats and combine.
Stir in raisins.
Roll into one or one-and-one-half-inch balls and arrange on ungreased baking sheet.
Bake at 375 degrees for eight or nine minutes.

Cocoa Kiss Cookies

We don't have a copy of Joan's recipe for these. Sometime in the dim past she gave it to Linda, so, the below recipe is that version.

Preheat oven to: 375 degrees

(**Note:** it is important to refrigerate the dough.)

Ingredients

2 cups (4 sticks) butter, softened

2/3 cup white sugar

1 teaspoon vanilla extract

1 2/3 cups all-purpose flour

1/4 cup unsweetened cocoa powder

1 cup chopped pecans

9-ounce bag chocolate kisses

1/3 cup confectioners' sugar for decoration

Directions

In mixer bowl, cream together the butter, sugar and vanilla.

Combine the flour and cocoa, add to the butter/sugar mixture and mix until all of the flour is absorbed. Stir in the pecans.

Cover and refrigerate dough for at least one hour.

Unwrap chocolate kisses. Mold about one tablespoon of dough around each chocolate kiss. Place one and one half inches apart on an ungreased cookie sheet.

Bake at 375 degrees for 10 to 12 minutes or until set.

Cool on the baking sheet for five minutes before removing to a wire rack to cool completely.

Roll cooled cookies in confectioners' sugar.

Thimble Cookies

(Notebook 10, pp 5 and cards #1)

Preheat oven to: 350 degrees

Ingredients:
1 cup sugar
1 cup shortening and 1/4 pound (one stick) butter or all shortening
2 egg yolks
1 tsp vanilla
3 cups flour
Jelly or jam

Directions:
In a mixer, cream the sugar and shortening (or butter). Add the egg yolks and vanilla and combine well.

Add the flour one cup at a time.

Roll into one-and-one-half-inch balls then press a thimble into the center of each, fill the hole with jelly or jam.

Bake at 350 degrees 8-10 minutes.

Drinks: (left to right) mai tais, whiskey sours and white Russian shakes

17 ▎

Drinks

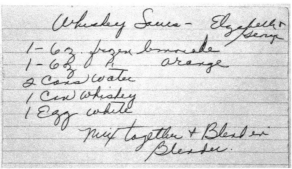

Whiskey Sours

(Notebook 11, pp 38 and Cards #2)

We found this recipe twice. In Joan's card box there is a notation that she got it from "Elizabeth and George."

Everyone in the family was amazed at how good these were. We chose Windsor Canadian Whiskey for the alcohol and it worked really well since it has no smoky flavors like bourbons do. That was an accidental discovery. We really chose Windsor because it was Joan's brother Bob Sell's favorite whiskey. Perhaps by coincidence, it's also quite inexpensive.

Ingredients:
6 oz frozen lemonade
6 oz frozen orange juice
12 oz water
6 oz whiskey (something that does not have a smoky flavor, Canadian Rye works well)
white of one egg
garnish with a Maraschino cherry

Direction:
Combine all the ingredients (except the cherry) in a blender and blend until frothy, about 20 seconds.

Pour into a pitcher then serve in individual whiskey sour glasses. Drop in a Maraschino cherry.

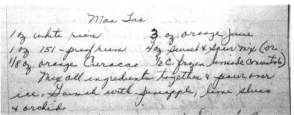

Mai Tai

(Notebook 11, pp 58)

This is Joan's recipe, but they were popular with Linda's first mother-in-law Kathleen Gartner, who always served them before Christmas dinner at her Flowertown home in the 1980s.

Linda described her:

> *Her maiden name was 'Bishop.' Her family was English and she made roast beef and York-*
> *shire pudding. She made cobbler with Bisquick and black cherries and served it with ice*
> *cream. She also made crown roasts with those little paper pantaloons.*
> *She had a Kitchen Aid mixer.*
> *She could sew really well and had a Bernina sewing machine and a dress form.*
> *Al's father worked in a hardware store and she worked for the state — the Bureau of Nar-*
> *cotics in Philadelphia.*

We used blue Curacao instead of orange and got delightfully colored green drinks.

Ingredients:
1 oz white rum
1 oz 151-proof rum
1/8 oz orange Curacao
3 oz orange juice
4 oz whiskey sour mix OR one fourth cup frozen limeade and one fourth cup water

Directions:
Combine all ingredients in a blender and pour into glasses.
Can be garnished with pineapple, lime slices and an orchid.

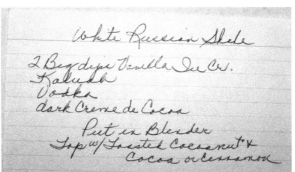

White Russian Shake

(Cards #3)

Linda never remembers Joan making these, but they're a great cocktail. We did make one major change. Joan's recipe called for a garnish of toasted coconut and cocoa or cinnamon. Using cocoa or cinnamon is a **serious choking hazard**. As you are about to take a sip of the drink you inhale the fine cocoa or cinnamon powder. The resulting cough generally results in a spray of the drink all over whatever is in front of you!

Shaved bittersweet chocolate or even mini chocolate chips are great substitutes.

Ingredients:
(drink)
2 cups vanilla ice cream
1 shot Kahlúa (chilled in freezer)
1 shot vodka (chilled in freezer)
1 shot dark Creme de Cocoa (chilled in freezer)
(topping)
3 tbsp toasted flake cocoanut OR
1/2 tsp shaved bittersweet chocolate

Directions:
Chill alcohols in freezer.

Chill glasses in freezer.

Toast cocoanut in frying pan until it just begins to turn brown then remove to a bowl to prevent burning.

Put drink ingredients in blender and blend until there are no longer any lumps of ice cream, 20-30 seconds. Do not over blend it if you want a thick milkshake consistency and not a liquid.

Pour into chilled glasses. Top with shaved bittersweet chocolate and/or toasted flaked coconut.

18

Rescuing Family Recipes

Recipes give us a way to travel in time.

The smells and tastes that we experienced earlier in life, especially our childhood and earliest adult years, come back vividly with just one whiff of the aromas or taste of a dish that was similar to one we loved.

This was famously explored in episode of the madeleine cookie in the first of the seven volumes of the *Remembrance of Things Past,* by the French writer Marcelle Proust (1871-1922). One of the foremost books of the Twentieth Century, it explores involuntary memory, which occurs in us when something we smell, taste or encounter automatically brings back memories.

The smell of pennyroyal mint will make my mind flash back to the dry shale path my brothers and I hiked on the ridge line behind our home town of Berwick, Pa. We knew there was a plant there that we were smelling. Possibly it flourished in the spring then dried out by the time we hiked over it, releasing that incredible fragrance. We could never find it. Many decades later while hiking on South Mountain near Carlisle, Pa., I smelled that same incredible mint scent and ask my hiking companion, a biology professor, what it was.

As a small child I always remember the wonderful steamy, butter-like smell that was pouring out of the kitchen of the Hotel Berwick next to the Presbyterian Church as we arrived early every Sunday morning. I assumed that it was butter and something sautéing in it. Decades later I walked into a friend's kitchen and smelled the same thing. "What is that?" I asked, explaining the involuntary memory of childhood Sunday mornings.

"I'm cooking down veal bones for stock," was the answer.

That made perfect sense since one of the first things one would expect to encounter in a professional kitchen in those days would be a simmering pot of veal bones creating the stock for use in the soups and sauces of the day.

The taste of mincemeat takes me to visions of large family Thanksgiving gatherings around my parents' dining room table.

I once ate at Haag's Hotel in Shartlesville, Pa., famous for Pennsylvania Dutch dinners. I walked in and was transported back to my grandmother's kitchen where chicken or beef pot pie had been cooking on a wood-fired plate stove.

This might be the chief reason to preserve family recipes. It gives you the opportunity to travel in time voluntarily or involuntarily. Once you get into the effort of saving them you will be surprised how many of the dishes evoke strong memories in other people in your family.

Recipes are one of the core parts of a family's culture. One generation's recipes in notebooks or file boxes can easily vanish as the years roll on. ANY method for recording and keeping the recipes for foods we love and value is good. Easier is better, since recipes often are passed from hand to hand and prepared on the fly. Most people do not have the time to make a full-blown, indexed archive of documents.

That said, it is also important to note – no matter how simply you preserve them – it is important to date recipes, to add a note about who or where they came from. And it is important to record the name of the person who is saving the recipe for posterity. At minimum, jot the information on sticky notes and attach them.

There are large numbers of incredibly interesting and valuable manuscript cookbooks, some hundreds of years old, in libraries and archives that have no names on them. I have two, one from 1896 and one from 1911.

Joan's file card boxes are full of cards with handwriting that is not hers. The beautiful scripts are clearly from a different age, how far back we just do not know.

To put this in perspective: Imagine that you have come into possession of a collection of recipes from an ancestor 100 or 150 years in the past. It would be thrilling to see how the dishes were prepared then with the technology of the day. It would be just as thrilling to know the year the recipe was written down and who captured it and where they lived and one or two details about their life.

At the beginning of your effort, no matter how modest or ambitions, consider that you might be reaching across time to a great-great grandchild in the far future. Tell them who you are, where you got the recipe, who gave it to you, when you got it and possibly what it meant to you. And, include your name and the town you lived in.

And yes, you can do all this on a computer, but scratching notes on a page in the kitchen is much easier than running to your machine or hauling out your phone to bring up the word-processing app. Also, the food stains on the pages are part of the charm and computers don't record them.

That said, the photo app in cell phone are absolutely invaluable for photographing the recipes you see in the magazines in the dentist's office or in somebody else cookbook. Upload them, print them out and put them in your kitchen notebook where they're ready for you to revise, add notes to and spill soy sauce on.

Since much of our food culture is recorded in the text and videos of Web sites, it can just as easily vanish when a site goes down. And, just as bad, there is such a vast volume of information available to us today, sometimes what we are looking for is simply lost in the glut.

Also, access to computerized records on home machines can be lost if the machine is damaged, lost, worn out or its owner passes away without leaving the system password. External hard drives are only good for about four years. One part of writing a will these days includes listing passwords for all machines and accounts.

Simply keeping recipes, and not keeping such a mass of them that you can't find anything in the piles, is half the battle. There was a phrase in the computer security world where I worked for many years, that described the process: "drinking from a firehose." It referred to the attempt to find anything in the mass of data that turned up whenever you turned a search tool loose on a very large data set (or the entire World Wide Web). You do need some discipline. You only need to keep what you really have cooked and like.

We have several friends who think that since we are ambitious cooks, we need copies of the dozens of new recipes that they encounter on the Web. The bulk of them go in the trash shortly after they come in the door.

I've been collecting cookbooks and recipes for many years, and I don't have a vast number of them. Certainly not the 1,400 recipes that Joan had. I've developed some methods (and seen what other people do) and I can recommend some practices to make the job easier.

1. Begin with one sturdy three-ring binder (write your name, address and date in the front) and label it "Recipes." Photo copy your most important family recipes, punch three holes in the pages and put them in the notebook. When you cook the recipe, add any notes to the page and put the date on top right of the page. Also, be sure to note where you got the recipe. Move the recipes you have cooked most recently to the front. This will result in your most favored recipes ending up near the front of the book. One way we remember things is by their recency — did I make that recipe last week or a year ago?

   As the years go by, the dated recipes will provide an interesting diary of what you were cooking and when. Date everything!!

   Cutting recipes out of newspapers and magazines and pasting them into a notebook has several problems: the glue lets go after a few years. Also, the paper they are printed on yellows and eventually crumbles — this is true in spades for clippings from newspapers. Photocopies of the articles, or print outs of recipes from the web last much longer.

   For recipes you think about keeping for posterity (or simply expect to make a lot) invest in better printer paper: 24-pound paper instead of the more inexpensive 20 pound.

2. Just as important as keeping your three-ring-binder, keep a good sturdy notebook to jot down recipes you create. And date them. And, as in the binders above, write your name and address and the date in the front.

   In my notebooks I make diary entries after each holiday meal that include how many people were at the meal, how many pounds of meat I bought, how long it took to roast the turkey, what new recipes I tried, what didn't prove to be too popular and what was a hit.

   Before I begin planning a holiday meal, I now can look back to the notes from previous years to refresh my memory on what to avoid and what to emphasize.

   I also keep a page for the year listing the new things I tried. This can be an interesting read in the future and a reminder of new recipes that you were fascinated by "then" that you might want to revisit.

In the backs of the notebooks, I devoted pages to lists of the foods and recipes that certain small (or large) children would eat (willingly). I found it interesting how the lists expanded as the years go on, and how the ex-boyfriends and ex-girlfriends have come and gone.

3. Try to collect your family's heirloom recipes and put them in a three-ring binder titled "Family Recipes." Unfortunately, we often don't go looking for those old recipes until a previous generation is gone. Then the hunt begins with the phone call: "do you have mom's recipe for that chocolate cake she used to make? Do you know if anybody else does?"

    This also is the place to put those recipes that you try out that are a major hit — NEW family food traditions.

4. You might as well start one notebook titled "Desserts." Humans being what they are, you're going to need it. Everyone LOVES sweets.

    I once read that the traditional housewife (19th and early 20th centuries) had about 20 recipes in her head and she made those over and over. The exception to that rule was desserts.

    I helped sort out a great-aunt's effects once after she passed away in the 1970s, and that was certainly true in her case. Aunt Alma was known to the family as a really, really good baker. She had dozens and dozens of cake, cookie and pastry recipes in her little file box. There was only ONE, recipe for something that wasn't a dessert. She obviously didn't need a recipe for the bulk of the meals she cooked.

5. Start a notebook for "other" recipes if you like ethnic or very modern cooking. I've always loved the cooking of Italy, Germany, Russia and Eastern Europe. As I come across recipes on the Web, in periodicals or in conversation with other people, I cook them and put the favorites in my "non-US" notebook with index tabs. We recently made some good friends who had come from Yorkshire in the north of England so there now is an "England" section too.

. . .

The most important thing to do is save what you have NOW and save it in a form that will last. At minimum, collect those treasured recipes and shove them in file folders for safe keeping.

Pick the 10 most important ones. Photocopy them and put them in a binder. Or, better yet, make copies for your siblings or your kids. Think of what this project will look like in 50 years. Date it. Write a bit of an introduction giving your name and town. The more copies you have out there in the family, the higher the chance that this little bit of your family history will survive.

Getting started even in the most modest way will make it feel less like you have an enormous job hanging over your head. That makes it easier to add recipes as you find them.

Self publishing

On the simplest scale, you can take a handful of hand written or printed pages to a printer, get an estimate, and have your recipes printed on sturdy paper stock and bound in a simple fashion.

One step up: type your recipes into a word processing program, design the pages in an artful way, scan (or photograph) the old family recipe cards and the finished dishes, then save it as a .pdf file and take that to your printer for an estimate. Having 20 copies printed for $20 each might seem like an expense, but not if you're going to give them as Christmas presents.

Go for it: Remember, anything you can put into a .pdf file can be turned into a book. Amazon and other Web-based self-publishing operations can turn out nice, soft bound books "on demand."

19

Appendix One — The Notebooks and File Boxes

Joan left a small library of 14 notebooks, three card file boxes of recipes, eight charity cookbooks and hundreds of magazine clippings There also were some small and intriguing premium cookbooks from 1918-1920 that might have belonged to her grandmother.

We numbered the notebooks and file card boxes for reference purposes and describe them below.

The oldest notebook

Possibly Joan was keeping a notebook of recipes before she expanded the scope of her recipe collecting. There are numerous recipes on loose pieces of lined notebook paper scattered throughout her later note books, clearly torn from an older notebook.

It appears that the oldest of Joan's notebooks is number 13 (our numbering system). It is a nine-and-one-half-by-six-inch, green Herald Square 75 sheet notebook sold by Woolworth, according to the cover. It cost 99 cents. Joan gave it no title, but on the top of the cover is written "Never stumble over something behind you."

Joan probably had reused an old notebook that she had used for her Tupperware dealer notes and household information. One of the back pages contains phone numbers for Al DeAngeleis and Al Jr. as well as notes "Spackle Ceiling" and "Call Bill Ingham UGI." UGI was her natural gas utility.

The book seems to be from the early 70s, When she started it, Joan was probably in a busy and stressful time of life. She was recently divorced from her first husband Kenneth Scheetz, Sr. (1969) and possibly remarried to Donald Knechel with four children (Linda, b. 1955; Ken Jr. b. 1957; Rick, b. 1962 and Tom, b 1965). She would have a fifth child, Chad, with her second husband Donald in 1972.

Linda remembers that Joan was a Tupperware dealer at that time and she clearly began using the notebook for her Tupperware sales work. There are three index tabs:

— "Notes from meetings"

— "Notes for coming parties"

— "Recipes"

In her papers there were numerous Tupperware handouts with recipes for Tupperware dealers. One page was titled: "Ever popular recipes for Party Demo." Another had "Recipes do sell Tupperware" underlined, at the top of a page.

The recipe entries at the back of notebook 13 begin with a mix of food and non-food, craft recipes: "Finger paints" then "Economy Brownie Mix" then "Christmas Clay."

Recipes for "Monkey Cake," "Watergate Cake" and "Watergate Salad" are among the 22 recipes recorded in her handwriting.

"Watergate" became a household word because of the scandal that followed the June 1972 break-in at the Democratic National Committee headquarters in the Watergate complex in Washington, D.C. About the same time, Kraft Foods had begun selling a bright green instant pistachio pudding mix and used a recipe "Pistachio Pineapple Delight" to promote the product. It is believed that an editor at a Chicago newspaper picked up the Kraft recipe and called it "Watergate Salad."[78]

According to the web site Atlas Obscura.com:

"By the 1970s, housewives transformed the salad into cake with the addition of white cake mix, vegetable oil, and club soda. They also swapped out the pineapple and mini marshmallows for pecans (or sometimes walnuts) and sweetened, dried coconut flakes. They frosted their finished creations with pistachio pudding–laced Dream Whip.

"Some time after President Richard Nixon resigned in 1974, both dishes were renamed Watergate Salad and Watergate Cake. "[79]

The notebooks and their dates

1. *Meat, chicken, fishcakes, vegetables and rice, pasta dishes, mac cheese* (**1957-2006**)
   Blue, spiral bound, Mead 70 sheet notebook, 10 1/2 x 8.
   Has "Salisbury Steak" written at top of cover.
   It contained a recipe for Deviled Clams next to an advertisement for Gold Seal linoleum with a copyright date of 1957. Linda said Joan loved deviled clams.
   Page 63, a recipe for Potato Casserole, has the note "Southern Living 99."
   It also contains a recipe that appears to have been printed out by a Giant grocery store source Nov. 24, 2006.

2. *One dish meals and soups cooking* (**1974-99**)
   Turquoise blue Mead 70 sheet notebook, 10 1/2 x 8.
   Contains page torn from unknown magazine with ad for The Pillsbury Company with a copyright date of 1974 and a clip from *Woman's Day* of Feb. 1, 1999.

3. *Pizza, calzones, lasagna; dips & sauces, marinades* (**1994**)
   Red, Mead 70 sheet notebook, 10 1/2 x 8.
   Contains a page of recipes from *Woman's Day*, Dec. 20, 1994, pp 116.

4. *#1 cakes; #2 cookies; pies* (**2005-06**)
   Red "Norcom Basic Notebook" 11 x 8 1/2-inch.
   Contains pages torn from *Redbook* magazine October, 2005, pp 230-232 and *Woman's Day*, Nov. 15, 2005 pp 143-6 and April 18, 2006, pp 110.

5. *Salads & dressings"* (**before late 1980s**)
   Plain tan cover (no back cover) 8 x 10 1/2 inches. The only possible dating information is the third from last recipe "Kristen's broccoli slaw salad." Assuming that is her son Tom's wife Kristen, the notebook would predate the time that Tom met Kristen: the late 1980s.

6. *1. Seafood; 2. hamburger and hamburger dishes* (**no date**)
   Green "Norcom Basic Notebook" 11 x 8 1/2 inches. Only contains one recipe: "Salmon Cakes w/ Lemon Herb Sauce" and a recipe clipped from a newspaper titled "Billy's Crab Patty Sandwiches."

7. *Snack mixes; #2 dips* (**no date**)
   Blue "Norcom Basic Notebook" 11 x 8 1/2 inches. Only contains two recipes.

8. *Cheesecakes* (**1993-2012**)
   Spiral bound, Green, Mead 70 sheet notebook, 10 1/2 x 8.
   Contains numerous clippings, including pages from *First*, Oct 11, 1993, pp 69-70; *Better Homes and Gardens*, Feb. 1995, pp 175-8; *Taste of Home*, Aug/Sept 1999, pp 167; *Woman's Day*, Nov. 19, 2002, pp 106 and Dec., 17, 2002, pp 194; *Woman's Day*, Feb.

13, 2007, pp 148; *Lehigh Valley Group* (newspaper) August, 23, 2007; *Allentown Morning Call,* August 22, 2012, *Life* section pp 1-2.

9. *Cookies, cakes, bread, baking tips* **(2002-07)**
Red and blue Stewart Hall, 10 1/2 x 8 notebook. Contains numerous clippings including a coupon that expired Jan. 19, 2002; a page from an *Allentown Morning* call April 21, 2004; the page of a calendar for December, 2004 (with recipe on back); clippings from page 214 and 210 of *Woman's Day,* Oct. 4, 2005; clipping from page 170 of *Woman's Day,* Nov. 15, 2005 and page 16 of *Parade* magazine July 15, 2007.
This appears to be the most used notebook. Its cover is ripped free and it is stuffed with the most clippings.

10. *Cookies* **(2002-11)**
Purple Norcom 70 sheet, one subject 10 1/2 x 8 inches.
A recipe for "Holiday Oatmeal Cookies" has the dates 2002 and 2011 to the left of the title. Another recipe for "Oatmeal Cookies" has a note: "Best of all Recipes 2004."
Possibly this was where she made a start on editing the recipes for her planned cookbook. This notebook is different than all the others. The recipes are all copied out in Joan's neat handwriting, sometimes two or three to the page. There is nothing pasted in the notebook and nothing crossed out. All the titles of the recipes are underlined with a red pen. Some have lines drawn around them. The above "Oatmeal Cookies" has an outline and an asterisk in addition to the note about "Best of..."

11. *Cakes and Pies & Puddings* **(2003).**
Plain blue cover (no back cover), wire spiral bound, 8 x 10 1/2 inches.
A section in the back is labeled "Salads & Dressings Dips Vegetables" It also contains three doodles, probably done by Chad, of a cylinder and two fantastic "horror" type characters with swords, one dripping blood.
It also contains recipes for various homemade wines pages 27-38.

12. *Pies & crusts; pudding and desserts* **(1990-2005)**
Spiral bound, dark blue, Mead 70 sheet notebook, 10 1/2 x 8.
Contains a booklet of 2004 Betty Crocker recipes from *Family Day* and a section from the *Doylestown Intelligencer* "The Fine Art of Cooking" dated October 4, 1990.

13. **Untitled (1977?)**
Herald Square 9 1/2 by 6-inch notebook. On cover: "Never stumble over something behind you" Contains notes for Tupperware sales activities, children's craft materials and 22 food recipes. Probably begun before 1977 when Joan sold Tupperware.

14. *Cookies* **(inside front cover)** *Candy* **(inside back cover). (no date)** Gregg steno book, 6 by 9 inch. Only contains three recipes.

The file boxes and their dates

#1. Florence's recipes with some from Suzanna. Dates 1949-1987 (possibly much earlier).
Wooden, 3 x 5 inches. Contained 208 cards and clippings.

There are two dated items in it providing a possible span of 1949 through 1987.

A newspaper clipping of a story "The Formula for Fastnacht success" contained a coupon for Jolly Time Popcorn with an expiration date of Sept. 30, 1987. There also was a recipe for "Casserole of Clams" on a card, the back of which contained a grid with headers containing the years 1949 through 1958.

We believe it belonged to Florence, Joan's mother. The box contained nine cards with Joan's name, five with "mother" (Susanne), two with the names of her sisters Estella and Molly and one with her grandson Ken Jr.'s nickname "Cork."

The box contains many cards that are yellowed, with a variety of handwriting and they seem older than the rest. Possibly those were from Joan's grandmother Susanne, who died in 1950, and were intermingled with Florence's cards.

Recipes with names of family members:

<u>Mother (Susanne)</u>
Strawberry Short Cake
Cheese Pie
Lemon Cake Pie
Baked Ham
Fried Apples
<u>Joan</u>
Joan's A.B. Cake

Lemon Lush
Brandy Pound Cake
Potato Chip Cookies
Chocolate Drops Non Parels
Pumpkin Pie
Salmon Croquettes
Cheese Balls
Peanut Butter Cake
<u>Cork (nickname for grandson Ken Jr.)</u>
Charcoaled Steaks Marinade"
<u>Estella and Molly (Florence's sisters)</u>
Pineapple Cake
Lemon Ice Cream

#2 Joan's recipes. Dates: 1970-2002

Metal 4 x 6 inches. Contained 342 cards and clippings, some cards were 3 x 5.

This appeared to have been Joan's main card box. There were many recipes that were familiar to Linda that Joan made frequently.

Dates:

— April, 1970

Small three panel brochure "Mixed Drink Recipes" published by the Pennsylvania Liquor Control Board.

— 1979

Recipe for "Broccoli Divan with Tuna" on back of a Century 21 calendar for February, 1979.

— Nov. 1980

Four-panel brochure *Recipes for Holiday Entertaining* published by the Pennsylvania Liquor Control Board.

— 1980-81

Small, 10-page *The BACARDI Party Book* containing drink and snack recipes.

— June 29, 1982

Tear sheet from *The Mercury* of Pottstown, pp A9-10 with a recipe for "Lemon Lush" and "Blueberry Buckle.

— 2002

Oct. 27, 2002, *Parade Magazine* recipe for "Deviled Salmon Cakes."

Recipes with names of family members:
<u>**Art (uncle)**</u>
Art's Apes Cake
<u>**Elsie**</u>
White AP Cake
Apes Cake
Roman Apple Cake

Jello Cake
<u>Linda (daughter)</u>
Chocolate Chip Cake
<u>Molly (aunt)</u>
Chocolate Fudge Cake
Beer Bread
Sweet Pickles
<u>Mom (Florence)</u>
Pumpkin Roll
Clam Chowder
<u>Mother</u>
Lemon Cake Pie
<u>Relda (aunt)</u>
Peanut Butter Marshmallow Eggs
<u>Stella (aunt)</u>
Stella's Apes Cake
Chocolate Peanut Butter Fudge
<u>Tom (Scheetz, son)</u>
Peanut Butter Crispy Eggs
Chocolate Brownies
<u>Tom (the author)</u>
Irish Soda Bread

#3 Joan's (new) recipes. Date: 2012
Plastic, 4 by 6 inches, contains 56 cards or clippings

This box is a mystery. The 56 cards were all neatly written in a consistent hand and showed no stains or signs of wear. There were some older recipes that we found in other boxes and notebooks. Most of the rest seemed to be the most modern recipes that Joan collected.

There is the possibility that it was a sort out of favored recipes.

Dates:
-- 2012
"Easy BBQ Short Ribs," Copyright 2012, Television Food Network

Recipes with names of friends or family members:
<u>Linda</u>
Tuna noodle
Linda's Dessert
<u>(Bobbie) Landes</u>
Broccoli slaw
White chili
<u>Rachel</u>
Hula Chicken

What would Joan's cookbook have looked like?

There is a certain order to traditional cookbooks that we copied to organize the sections of Joan's notebooks to see what her table of contents might have looked like. Some notebooks had more than one major section. Two had very few recipes in them. Below is our best guess:

Salads and Dressings Notebooks 5 and 11
Soup Notebook 2
Meat Notebook 1
Fish Notebook 1
Casseroles Notebook 2
Italian Recipes Notebook 3
Vegetables Notebook 1 and 11
Breads and Muffins Notebook 9
Cakes Notebook 9 and 11
Cookies Notebook 9 and 10
Pies Notebook 11 and 12
Puddings Notebook 12
Cheese Cakes Notebook 8
Dips and Sauces Notebook 3 and 11
Drinks and Winemaking Notebook 11

Two things stand out when we look at that conjectural table of contents.

The first is that Notebook 11 contained a wider variety of recipes than the other notebooks. It looks older and more tattered than most of the others. Its front cover was obviously lost so long ago that Joan moved the blue back cover around to the front (it's spiral bound) and wrote *Cakes and Pies & Puddings* on it.

The second thing that stands out is the large number of Italian recipes that she collected in Notebook 3. There are 12 recipes in that notebook including several each for calzones, lasagnas, pizzas and frittata (as well as a recipe for a "Skillet Tamale Pie" from Woman's Day magazine that she apparently considered "* excellent").

20

Appendix Two — Charity and Premium Cookbooks

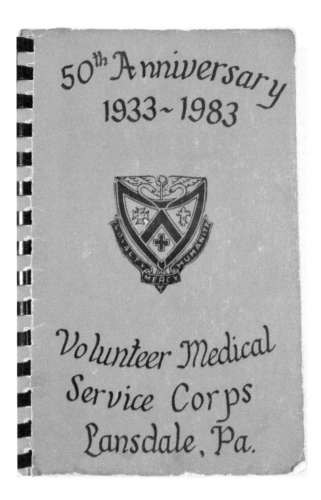

50th Anniversary 1933-1983 Volunteer Medical Service Corps Lansdale, Pa, 1983, charity cookbook.

Many of Joan's family's recipes were preserved in a 1983 charity cookbook published by the Volunteer Medical Service Corps of Landsdale, Pa. It was published for the group's 50th anniversary and printed by the Funcraft Published of Pleasanton, Kan. On the title page someone wrote the date May 7, 1983.

Joan's aunts Estella (Rothenberger) Gift and Marion (Rothenberger) Taylor and her mother Florence (Rothenberger) Sell, were active with the group (especially Marion, who was a nurse) and contributed recipes to it. They solicited recipes from Linda as well. Their names are printed with the recipes, as in most charity cookbooks (Marion, 9; Estella, 6; Florence, 5; Joan, 5 and Linda, 5). There are 511 recipes in the book.

Joan gave copies to each of her children. Linda owns two copies, one used so heavily through a lifetime of cooking that it exists only as a pile of worn pages.

The Heirloom Cookbook, 1975, charity cookbook published by the Quakertown Historical Society, 1975. The last pages contain advertisements for eight Quakertown area banks, suggesting that their sponsorship paid for the printing. In the front of the volume a paragraph briefly describes the project and says it "was an effort to preserve the many fine old recipes that reflect our area's heritage" and to raise funds to aid in the restoration of the 1812 Burgess-Foulke house, home of the first burgess of Quakertown.

We have two copies, Linda's and Joan's. Joan's is inscribed inside the front cover with her name and the date Jan. 1, 1976.

Joan wrote a recipe for bacon dressing in this and it also contained a recipe for Drop Doughnuts torn from a publication. The fragment containing the recipe also had the printed address:

Scheetz, Kenneth A.

120 N. Main St.

Trumbauersville, Pa.

The recipe might be older than the cookbook since the address contained no zip code. Zip codes came into use in the U.S. in 1963.

Home Cookin' — Christ Lutheran Church, 2004, charity cookbook (Kulpsville, Pa.) This is nearly new and didn't appear to have been used. It's a great cookbook though with some very interesting recipes. Somehow it seems like the kind of recipes that Joan would have been attracted to.

Many of the recipes are from a time after the period of Joan's favored time (1950-70), however, there are many familiar older dishes that she has in her collection.

It contains a recipe for "Meatballs and Grape Jelly" (pp 8) — an appetizer of meatballs in a sauce of chili sauce and grape jelly that was at every party I attended in the early 1970s.

It also contains at least three recipes that call for Hidden Valley Ranch Dressing. That salad dressing was invented in the early 1950s by Steve and Gayle Henson on their dude ranch in Santa Barbara County, Calif. Initially they just sold it to guests, but then set up a manufacturing facility to sell it regionally, then nationwide. In 1972 it was bought by Clorox. The Hidden Valley website, at this writing, provides 766 recipes that use their products.[80] A search function allows a visitor to search by ingredient.

The Lutheran cookbook also has a recipe for Funny Cake (pp 110, one of Joan's family's favorites) and Potato Chip Cookies (pp 123) that is quite similar to those we found in Joan's and Florence's recipes. Both seem to be regional recipes.

The Bisquick Cookbook, Recipes from Betty Crocker in answer to your requests, 1964, premium cookbook

This is a 112-page, hard cover, spiral-bound premium cookbook. "Joan" is written inside the front cover. There were two Post-it notes containing recipes for Yellow Cake and Silver (white cake).

Betty Crocker Bisquick Family Favorites, 2001, premium cookbook, 32-page, staple bound.

Farm and Home Almanac, Southeastern Pennsylvania Edition, 1956, for-profit publication containing many recipes as well as advertising and other features, staple bound. This is a fragment, missing the front of the book and covers. (See description below.)

Farm and Home Almanac, Pa, Dutch Recipes & Dictionary Southeastern Pennsylvania Edition, 1958, for-profit publication containing many recipes as well as advertising and other features, staple bound.

In good condition. 84 pages (not numbered.) Every left side page contained advertising. It includes pages listing all the office holders in Bucks, Lehigh, Montgomery and Northampton counties.

The 1958 edition contains an "English-Penna. German Vocabulary" and the editors noted that the feature started in the 1957 edition.

The price of 25 cents was printed on the cover and it was listed as "A Meriedith Publication."

The Meredith Corporation of Des Moines, Iowa, describes itself today as "the nation's leading media and marketing company." It's a multi-media publishing company that has been in business for 110 years.

Good Housekeeping's Meat Cookbook, 1958, Published by Good Housekeeping Magazine, 68 pages, soft cover.

Charity cookbook fragment #1. no date. Contains pages 3 through 188. Some notes written on recipes throughout.

Charity cookbook fragment #2. no date. Side staple bound. Contains pages 7 through 140. Some notes written on recipes throughout. Each recipe is followed by the name of the contributor — evidence that it is a charity cookbook. It doesn't seem to have many "Dutch" recipes in it, although there is a very good description of how to make and can sauerkraut (submitted by Mrs. James B. Rutledge, pp 122)

A recipe for Shoo Fly pie is spelled "Shu-Fly pie" (submitted by Mrs. Elmer Slade, pp 111). The Boiled Water Pie Crust (submitted by Mrs. G. Howard Slade, pp 103) has a check mark beside it. It's the same as the Rothenberger pie crust recipe.

The book also has a recipe for "Harrisburg Cake," (submitted by Blanche R. Slade, pp 62), suggesting that the cookbook probably originated in Pennsylvania.

Goodhousekeeping's Poultry & Game Book, no date, premium cookbook. Soft cover, staple bound. 68 pages.

The Schwenkfelder Cookook, 1973, charity cookbook. Spiral bound, 128 pages.

The front cover contains the description: "Compiled by the Ladies' Aid Society of the Schwenkfelder Church, Palm, Pa., containing many recipes of Pennsylvania Dutch origin."

It contains nine recipes for Apies cake, none matching Joan's favored one.

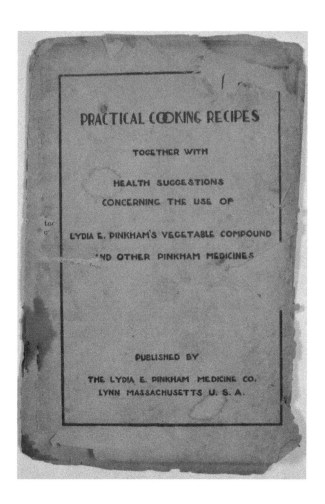

Practical Cooking Recipes together with health suggestions concerning the use of Lydia E. Pinkham's Vegetable Compound and other Pinkham Medicines, 1920, premium cookbook, very brittle 4 1/2-by-7-inch fragment.

This was published by the Lydia E. Pinkham Medicine Co., Lynn, Mass. Web sources list its publication date as 1920.[81]

Lydia Pinkham's Vegetable Compound was a very popular 19th Century herbal quack cure for "women's complaints." It was 15 percent alcohol and ran into marketing difficulties after the passage of the Pure Food and Drug Act in 1906. The Act required that ingredients to be disclosed on product labels. The company changed its formula, reducing the amount of alcohol, at that point but continued to sell the product.

Company ads urged women to write to Lydia. Women did write and they received answers for decades after Pinkham died in 1883. The answers, written by the staff, contained advice about women's medical issues and recommendations that they use the company product.

In 1905, the *Ladies' Home Journal* published a photograph of Pinkham's tombstone showing that she had been dead for the previous 12 years and exposed the fraud (Wikipedia). The company continued to sell the herbal product and it still can be found, although not the original recipe. The cookbook we have contains advertising on nearly every page scattered among the recipes.

The Metropolitan Life Cookbook, 1918,[82] Premium cookbook.

"for the use of industrial policy holders." The 63 pages are probably the entire book since there is a title page at the beginning and index at the end. This apparently was widely distributed. Its text is available on the web and copies are being sold from a number of outlets.

Taste of Home, February/March 2003 issue. The magazine is full of recipes and feature stories and includes a 16-page center tear-out section of recipes submitted by readers.

Taste of Home Savings Pack, 2002, premium recipe and coupon booklet, 32 pages. This contains 12 "clip and keep" recipes in 3 1/2-by-4 1/2 inch, double-sided format in addition to many pages of advertising with some recipes in the ads. Since there is a holiday theme to the advertising, it probably was published late in 2002. Coupons expire in 2003. Advertisers include Ocean Spray, Karo, Nestle, Hormel, Tyson, Campbell's and Jell-O.

Cook's Illustrated, 2003 undated magazine, 32 pages, 9 x 11 inches. This publication is full of cooking "technique" feature stories and product ratings. the ratings included a survey of frozen French fries that concluded they were all "not recommended" except Alexia Gourmet Quality Oven Fries, which were rated "not awful."

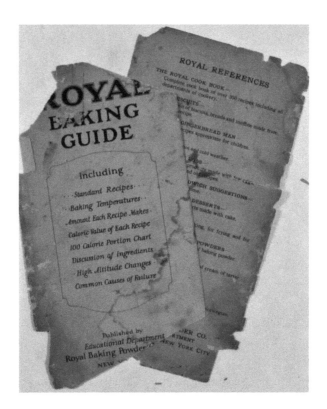

Royal Baking Guide, no date, four-page pamphlet published by the Royal Baking Powder Company, New York, NY.

This may have been a package insert with advice on using the product and a list of 12 "Royal References" — apparently books that could be mail ordered from the company — including a "Jewish Cook Book" and "Foreign Cookbooks" which included French, German, Spanish, Italian, Japanese, Norwegian, Portuguese Swedish and Chinese.

Kraft Food and Family, Spring 2007 magazine, 68 pages, published by Kraft test kitchens. The issue contains advertising and recipes that use Kraft products, including the venerable seven-layer bean dip.

The quarterly magazine is still available: $13.98 per year from the company's Website.[83]

21

Appendix Three — Other Historic Family
Recipes

Sauerkraut

    Sauerkraut, a Pennsylvania Dutch staple, has been eaten for more than 1,000 years in central and eastern Europe, the Balkans and Russia. It is simply salt-fermented cabbage. Until late in the Ninteenth Century in parts of Europe it was made by submerging whole heads of cabbage in brine and letting them ferment.

The cabbage leaves were then pulled off and "stuffed" with a variety of fillings, or sliced thinly and cooked.

I've made 20-30 quarts of sauerkraut each fall for many years.

A 2005 entry in my notebook indicates I canned 27 quarts that year. Cabbage was $.16 per pound. I shave it as thinly as possible with an Austrian-made Silvretta cabbage shredder and ferment it in crocks for five or six weeks starting in October.

Since the fermented sauerkraut is acidic and salted, it can be canned using a water-bath canning process— bringing the sauerkraut to a boil, then filling the jars, sealing them and water-bath canning them for 25 minutes for quart jars (20 minutes for pints).

I once experimented with pickling the whole heads using directions from a Bosnian friend who operates a small market a short distance from my home.

She told me to cut the hearts out of the cabbage, fill the remaining hole with pickling salt, let the heads stand for 24 hours. Cover them with brine (one tablespoon of pickling salt to one quart of water) and ferment them for the five to six weeks (the same as kraut made with shaved cabbage). She said you also can put them in the bottom of a crock and cover them with shaved cabbage when you make kraut the normal way. I've done it both ways.

The leaves were very interesting as wrappers for stuffed cabbage (also called halupki, gołąbki or pigeons), but when shaved as thinly as possible and cooked, the result was a much tougher sauerkraut than that made by shaving it first. Fermenting shaved cabbage is a big improvement.

A friend, Dr. William J. Morrison, a retired biology professor from Shippensburg University, spent a sabbatical in Vilnius, Lithuania in the 1980s while that country was still part of the Soviet Union. He said that life there was quite sparse. Bar food in Vilnius at that time was either a bowl of cooked (dried) peas, or whole, pickled cabbage leaves, which the locals called "Moscow pickle." It sounded to me like sauerkraut made the ancient way.

Footnotes

1. https://www.nytimes.com/2018/10/24/obituaries/dorcas-reilly-dead-green-bean-casse-role.html
2. Cannon, Poppy *The Can-Opener Cookbook,* (New York: McFadden Books, 1952), 7
3. http://rebeccaruth.stores.yahoo.net/100proofbour1.html
4. https://www.kelchnershorseradish.com/about/our-company/ (accessed 2/2019)
5. https://www.silverspringfoods.com/heritage/historical-timeline (accessed 2/2019)
6. Smith, ed., *The Oxford Encyclopedia of Food and Drink in America,* (New York: Oxford University Press, 2004), Vol. 1, 587
7. *The Brooklyn Sunday Sun*, Brooklyn, New York, Dec 28, 1873, 6
8. *Lancaster New Era*, Lancaster, Pa., Sept. 05, 1885, 5
9. Kander and Schoenfeld, ed., *1903 Settlement Cookbook* (New York: Gramercy Publishing Company, Facsimile Edition, 1987), 46
10. Farmer, Fannie Merritt, *The Boston Cooking School Cookbook,* (Baltimore: Oppenheimer Publishers, Inc., Facsimile edition, 2000), 124
11. Kiple, Kenneth F., Ed., *Cambridge World History of Food* (Cambridge, England: Cambridge University Press, 2000), 1878
12. Smith, *The Oxford Encyclopedia of Food and Drink in America*, Vol. 1, 198.
13. Weaver, William Woys, *Pennsylvania Dutch Country Cooking,* (New York: Abbeville Press, 1993), 53
14. Goldstein, Darra *A La Russe*, (New York: Random House, 1983), 204
15. Smith, *The Oxford Encyclopedia of Food and Drink in America*, Vol. 1, 564
16. Smith, *The Oxford Encyclopedia of Food and Drink in America*, Vol. 1, 732
17. https://genius.com/William-bolcom-lime-jell-o-marshmallow-cottage-cheese-surprise-lyrics
18. http://www.stlukeselca.com/youmightbealutheranif.htm
19. Weaver, William Woys, *Sauerkraut Yankees* (Philadelphia: University of Pennsylvania Press, 1983), 151.
20. http://www.knaussfoods.com/about-us.html
21. Smith, *The Oxford Encyclopedia of Food and Drink in America*, Vol. 1, 491
22. Farmer, *The Boston Cooking School Cookbook*, 308-312
23. Weaver, *Sauerkraut Yankees*, xv
24. General Mills, Inc., *The Bisquick "No Time to Cook" Recipe Book featuring Impossible Pies*, (Minneapolis, Minn.: General Mills, Inc., 1982), 4
25. Weaver, *America Eats*, (New York: Harper & Row Publishers, 1989), 57

26. https://www.prismnet.com/~wallen/chili/antique.html (accessed Feb. 2019)

27. https://www.nytimes.com/2007/08/24/arts/music/24park.html

28. Smith, *The Oxford Encyclopedia of Food and Drink in America*, Vol. 1, 230-233

29. Smith, *The Oxford Encyclopedia of Food and Drink in America*, Vol. 1, 253

30. http://www.thejoykitchen.com/recipe/cincinnati-chili-cockaigne

31. https://www.creamette.com/en-us/content/27330/OurStory.aspx

32. https://en.wikipedia.org/wiki/Spatini_sauce (accessed Feb. 2019)

33. https://topsecretrecipes.com/spatini-spaghetti-sauce-mix-copycat-recipe.html

34. Kelchner, Tom, *Kitchen Notebook 1*, (unpublished, 1992-97), 103.

35. https://en.wikipedia.org/wiki/Poppy_Cannon (accessed Feb. 2019)

36. https://www.kraftrecipes.com/member-recipe/00122408/lemon-lush

37. Freeman, Marjorie, et. al.; *The Educated Palate* (Chambersburg: privately printed, Penn Hall Alumnae, 1973)

38. *Fort Worth Star-Telegram*, Fort Worth, Tex., Jan, 23, 1956, 3

39. *The Atlanta Constitution*, Atlanta, Georgia, Jan, 25, 1960, 18

40. *Detroit Free Press*, Detroit, Mich., Mar 23, 1966, 31

41. Weaver, *Pennsylvania Dutch Country Cooking*"

42. Weaver, *Pennsylvania Dutch Country Cooking,* 18

43. Roan, Nancy, et al, *Boyertown Cookery*, (Boyertown: Boyertown Historical Society 1978), 56

44. Smith, *The Oxford Encyclopedia of Food and Drink in America*, Vol. 1, 217

45. Simmons, Amelia *American Cookery* (Harriman Tenn.: Pioneer Press, 1796, 1966 reprint), 33-34

46. Smith, *The Oxford Encyclopedia of Food and Drink in America*, Vol 1, 641

47. Ibid, 356

48. *Evening Sun*, Baltimore, Md., Nov 27, 1968, 14

49. *Philadelphia Inquirer*, Philadelphia, Pa., Nov 07, 1968, 15

50. *Intelligencer Journal*, Lancaster, Pa., Aug 04, 1969, 4

51. *Daily Record*, Long Branch, N.J., Sep 17, 1969, 6

52. Leonard, Leah, *Jewish Cookery*, (New York: Crown Publishers, 1949)

53. https://en.wikipedia.org/wiki/Jewish_apple_cake (accessed March 2020)

54. *The Terre Haute Tribune*, Terre Haute, In., Apr 3, 1960, 44

55. *The Miami Herald*, Miami, Fla., Mar 27 1962, 71

56. Crownover, Mary, *Cheesecake Extraordinaire* (New York, N.Y., Contemporary Books) 1994

57. Kiple, Kenneth F., ed., *Cambridge World History of Food*, Vol. 2, pp 1220

58. Pennsylvania State Grange Home Economics Committee, *Pennsylvania State Grange Cook Book,* (Harrisburg, Pa.: Pennsylvania State Grange 1950), 186.

59. Rombauer, Irma S., *The Joy of Cooking* (1931 facsimile edition) (New York, Simon & Schuster, Inc. 1998), 211

60. Smith, *The Oxford Encyclopedia of Food and Drink in America*, Vol. 1, 19

61. Weaver, *American as Shoofly Pie, The Folklore and Fakelore of Pennsylvania Dutch Cuisine"* (Philadelphia: University of Pennsylvania Press, 2013)

62. Pennsylvania State Grange Home Economics Committee, *Pennsylvania State Grange Cook Book,* 183-4

63. Weaver, *Pennsylvania Dutch Country Cooking,* 96

64. Wayes, Connie, et al, *The Heirloom Cookbook,* (Quakertown, Pa.: Quakertown Historic Society, 1975) 148

65. Smith, Ed., *The Oxford Encyclopedia of Food and Drink in America,* Vol. 1, 563.

66. Kiple, Kenneth F., ed., *Cambridge World History of Food*, Vol. 2, pp 1843

67. Smith, *The Oxford Encyclopedia of Food and Drink in America*, Vol. 2, 361

68. Gastronomic Committee, Larousse Gastronomique (New York: Random House, 2001 edition), 749

69. Ibid, pp 756

70. Simmons, Amelia, *American Cookery*, 16

71. Harold McGee, *On Food and Cooking,* (New York: Scribner, revised first ed., 2004), 708

72. Smith, *The Oxford Encyclopedia of Food and Drink in America*, Vol. 2, 246

73. Smith, *The Oxford Encyclopedia of Food and Drink in America*, Vol. 1, 318

74. Kiple, Kenneth F., ed., *Cambridge World History of Food*, Vol. 1, pp 365

75. Steven Poses, et al, *Frog Commissary Cookbook*, (New York: Doubleday, 1985), 252

76. https://en.wikipedia.org/wiki/Frog_Commissary#cite_note-3 (accessed March 2020)

77. Smith, *The Oxford Encyclopedia of Food and Drink in America*, Vol. 1, 309

78. https://www.seriouseats.com/2011/06/watergate-salad-nuts-pineapple-marshmallows-pecans.html

79. https://www.atlasobscura.com/foods/watergate-cake-pistachio

80. https://www.hiddenvalley.com/recipe/

81. Copies are available for sale by Amazon.com: https://www.amazon.com/Practical-Cooking-Recipes-Pinkham-Medicine/dp/B000VO6FZY

82. Full text available at archive.org https://archive.org/stream/metlifecookbook00metruoft/metlifecookbook00metruoft_djvu.txt

83. https://www.kraftrecipes.com/

Recipe index

Index

About the author

Tom Kelchner is married to the late Joan Knechel's daughter Linda. He worked in a variety of careers including newspaper journalism and as deputy press secretary to former Pennsylvania Governor Robert P. Casey. He also worked as a malicious code and malicious Website analyst, technical writer and blogger for ICSA Labs of Mechanicsburg, Pa., and the computer anti-virus threat research groups of Earthlink, Sunbelt Software and AVG.

He has had a life-long interest in cooking and baking the foods of many countries and regions including those of Russia, Europe, the British Isles, the Balkans, U.S. and the Caribbean.

He and his wife are descended from Pennsylvania Dutch families with roots in northern Pennsylvania and the Lehigh Valley.

He blogs about the "food and drink of everyday life" at PaFoodLife.com and the companion Facebook group PaFoodLife.